Objective Look

A Critical Look at Our Society's Lifestyle

Written by: M. M. Nourbakhsh
Edited by: H. Zavosh and
M. Inbody, Senior Editor,
Black Forest Press

PUBLISHED IN THE UNITED STATES OF AMERICA
BY BLACK FOREST PRESS
January, 2002
First Edition
P.O.Box 6342
Chula Vista, CA 91909-6342

**Cover Design
by Penni and Dale Neely.**

Unless with its author's written permission, this book is not to be reproduced in any modified or other edited form, nor any portion thereof being broadcasted or printed for reproduction or publication of any kind. It has to remain in its original complete form and be published with its author's approval.

Printed in the United States of America
Library of Congress
Cataloging-in-Publication

ISBN: 1-58275-070-X

Copyright © October, 1998; May, 2000; January, 2002;
by
Mahmoud M. Nourbakhsh, M.D.

This book is dedicated to
the society's better people all over the world,
those who have died, those who are living,
and the ones who have not yet been born.

Table of Contents

A Note from the Author

This is not a book to read for fun or entertainment, but one that contains a variety of very important and serious subjects of discussion. After reading it all, from beginning to the end, you may draw your own sensible conclusions on how we should try to improve adequately our society's lifestyle.

There is one very important remark or request that I have for people, and I wish I could make the world hear this: We have problems generated in every part of the world through group prejudice. When two other unpleasant qualities, namely greed and selfishness, are added to the variety of group prejudices that people have, then we can observe the serious detrimental outcomes everywhere.

Unfortunately, our society's lifestyle and present civilization somehow keep encouraging group prejudice. This can be observed in the areas of religious affiliations, sport competitions, and excessive national, racial, or professional ambitions, and through formation of groups for the purpose of organized activities in politics, finances, and other aspects of our social function.

If we do not try to eliminate presentation of unwise prejudice with dislike towards others, as individuals or groups, we may continue to keep the people of this planet, including our descendants and those of others who are very dear to us, in constant struggle to survive against our self-generated difficulties.

1

The Opening Chapter

God Almighty, please help us make use of this book as a service to humanity.

Hopefully the readers of the book will forgive the shortcomings of the language, since I am an immigrant to America and learned to speak English as an adult. As I live in this part of the world the book is written in English, and the critical look is directed mainly towards our western society. This is not to result in any comparative conclusion. I have, by free choice, elected to reside in this country, hoping that it continues to be a land of opportunities for generations to come.

After having lived in different parts of the world, amongst various cultures, now, in my old age, I would like to share with others some of the views and opinions developed as a result of the experiences of my life.

One of the most important aspects of our civilization is the recording of the results of experiments made in order that they may be studied and used by others. If this is true in the case of scientific and technical projects, perhaps it would be even more valuable when recording the essence of the experiences of a person's whole life. This may help the younger generation in learning how to make proper use of their time, by taking better advantage of their vast knowledge and capabilities.

When we want to differentiate between good and bad or right and wrong in our life and society, we need to try very hard to be logical, keeping our emotions, personal concerns and prejudice controlled, at least for a period of time.

Through this book and its contents, I am not trying to establish a new way of life, nor am I offering any new knowledge. I am certainly not claiming to have a special quality or qualification that would make me capable of writing any above average book. As a very ordinary person, concerned about my observations of the life of our generation, I am merely trying to present to the readers some of my personal understandings on the various concepts of our life in this world. Furthermore, I discuss and present my personal views in distinguishing the rights and wrongs, offering some reasons on why we should try courageously to be good, to do right, and to strive towards perfection.

I share with you my views, hopefully as free from bias as possible, on the life of our society, considering my observations of a vast variety of people, having lived amongst and with them. I want not only to criticize, but also to make constructive and logical suggestions on what is reasonable to be done.

I do not have any proficiency in the sciences of sociology, politics and religion, though some discussions in this book will involve these fields of study.

As you are reading this book, please allow your final evaluation to be made only after you have read it all. You are also requested to set aside from the beginning, any racial, national, political, religious, professional, or other bias that you may have, permitting yourself to read the book with an open mind and making a fair evaluation and judgment at its conclusion.

In this book I shall discuss a variety of subjects, at times almost jumping to different branches. I hope, by the time you finish reading it, you can synthesize the content and the branches together, possibly forming a useful tree. In the latter part of the book, I make reference to the example of this tree with qualities, hopefully, related to it.

As I am sincere in presenting my personal feelings or views to the reader, please do not expect me to prove my suggestions or to present evidence in their support. I am simply offering some thoughts and experiences, with good intention, for the well-being of our society.

While reading, please expect to see some statements or items of discussion being intentionally or unintentionally repeated in different parts of this book.

2

Life on Earth

The planet earth is a functioning unit. We are as living cells of this body. If any cell or group of cells malfunctions and disregards the adequate cooperation needed for present and future well-being of this planet, some damage to the process of function can be expected. The individual cells of this large unit ought not to strive selfishly for their own survival without respect for the needs of others. This is more important in the case of groups and larger groups and may be compared to parts of tissues and organs of a living animal or human being. If some part stops performing its duties and, more seriously, if it functions against some other parts, the outcome may affect the whole body, causing an illness. This can be minor and transient or major with serious future complications.

3

Our Home and Us

When family members or a large group of people live together in one house, they have mutual interest in everything related to life in their home.

The proper maintenance of the building, the adequate function of its utilities, the matters related to health and hygiene, the supply of food and other necessities, the atmosphere of peace and tranquility, and many other factors related to that house, to the living conditions within it, and towards its future safety and stability, are all of utmost importance to everyone who lives there.

There should exist cooperation among the group, in observation of the general rules, with consideration and respect towards the common interests of all concerned. If a member tries to take advantage of the others in a selfish manner, the whole family or group would suffer from the consequences.

The results of the deeds and behavior of every member of the group, whether right or wrong, will have much more effect on the ones who are closer to that person, but can cause, in some way, good or bad influence on the life of the whole group, including the one who has been the source of that action.

We are a large family, living on the surface of this planet, tied and attached to each other with many invisible strings. Among us there seem to exist a wide range and strata of human qualities and behavioral characteristics. At one extreme we can find individuals who are prepared to literally sacrifice themselves for the sake of others and for the betterment of the life of the society. On the other extreme we may see others who cause any degree of damage or injury to their community to satisfy their own pleasure and selfish physical, emotional, or even imaginary gains. Of course, the majority belong to the innumerable levels of qualities in between the extremes.

As we belong to a universal society, being part of the wide world of human life, we should have rules that support the society and its prosperity.

We have to provide continuous encouragement for the ones who are striving towards the future integrity of the society. At the same time we should obviously discourage any potential of damage to the society living on this planet.

4

For a Better Coming

The future is more important than the past. We use the past to satisfy our present and establish insurance for our future. Time keeps moving on. Before long, what is present will be past. Then it becomes out of reach, so that we will not be able to change it any more, except in our memory and imagination. In fact, at every moment of time the present is already reached, so it is only the future that we may control or change.

If we are happy or sad due to some past event, that is again because of our concern for the future. When there is much joy from having successfully passed a difficult test, or having found or bought a beautiful house or a nice car, or having been appointed to a desired position, it is all for the pleasure of the use of these in the future. On the other hand, if we are in deep sorrow due to the demise of a loved one, our sadness is due to not being able to have the presence of that individual any more in the future.

If we learn to be pleased at every step of the time with our efforts to improve the future, we can expect twofold satisfaction. At every stage we may feel the satisfaction of having made adequate use of the past without wasting it, while at the same time enjoy a feeling of expectation at every moment for a better future.

It is logical to accept that joy and satisfaction can become multifold if all members of the society learn to be pleased at all times with their efforts to improve not only their own future but also the future of others and society as a whole.

5

The Young and the Old

In a healthy society there should exist an adequate intimacy among different age groups. The socialization of different age groups with each other, whether family members or friends, if done correctly and with mutual respect, will be beneficial to the young as well as the old.

As we reach old age, having contact with the young and a very young society will have re-energizing effect on us. In old age it is also very essential and helpful to feel that we are still useful to some people, to sense that we are not deserted, to see that they pay attention to us and, at the time when we no longer are as capable as we were in our youth, to have those who hold our hand and show us affection while asking our opinion or advice on serious matters. They may even let us feel that, at least at times, what we say is of benefit to others. They can show us that if our diminished physical capabilities do not let us compete with the young world any more, our mental abilities, in spite of their deterioration and weakening, can be used to advantage in society due to reinforcement received during our long years of experience.

For the older generation to be convinced that this is in fact real, and to enhance their self-confidence, extra energy will be derived from loving concern, encouragement and confidence given by the younger generation. As a result of this generational interaction, a beneficial cycle or chain of events will evolve. The encouraged older person who has hopes and still an adequate will to live, for whatever period of time, would become happier and develop courage for greater physical activities that will result in a better appetite and improved function of the digestive, respiratory and circulatory systems. This may, in turn, result in improvement of that person's mental efficiency or memory and, as an outcome, a better relationship with society. In response, more encouragement can be expected from society, both family and others, with hopes for continuation of this happy chain of reactions.

The young ones will gain a twofold benefit from their adequate and proper association with the older age group. On the one hand, they can take advantage of the abundance of information on many subjects with appropriate guidance on how to make decisions on important issues in their lives. They can benefit from the opinion of those who have already passed through the same stages of life, imparting firsthand knowledge on their personal experiences. They give advice that can be trusted with confidence, as with their gray hair there possibly exists some wisdom that could be acquired only in exchange for precious years of life. On the other hand, through their observation of the other extreme of life, the young ones, when watching the elders who are loved and respected, will be more hopeful of prosperity in their own old age. When those of the younger generation notice that the old ones are content with their status, being part of the society, joining others in some festive activities and gatherings, having some useful presence and presentable character, they, in turn, may feel consciously and subconsciously much more contentment with their lives and more optimism towards the distant future.

6

All Together and in Harmony

We are living in a beautiful world with an unlimited supply of goods at our disposal. There is such an abundance of bounties of different kinds made available to us by our Creator that we do not appreciate, recognize, or even notice, except a very small fraction of these bounties. If, through cooperation with each other, we make appropriate use of these resources, we may find in them the needed ingredients for an adequate level of happiness for mankind on this planet. But if individually and as groups, we try to take selfish advantage of portions of this wonderful supply, inconsiderate of the rights of others, sooner or later we will cause a decline in the degree of comfort and increase stress and sufferings for everybody, including ourselves and the ones who are dear to us, both of the present and future generations.

7

cA Couple of cAttractions

I remember having heard the remark that children are attracted to two objects that can be extremely dangerous, but with which they very much like to play: fire and water. We should caution them strongly to avoid the former, as it has particular uses but is not a toy. They need, at the same time, to be taught how to play safely with the other one. When the latter is used wisely, it is a necessity for life and much fun to play with. If, on the other hand, it is dealt with carelessly, it can be a killer.

In a similar way, later on, and through the early years of adolescence, we may observe their affinity towards two powerful attractions. One, with the application of our patient support and their own developing wisdom and foresight, they should learn to keep away from. This is the use of habit-forming and harmful substances such as cigarettes, drugs without medical indication, and most particularly alcoholic beverages. They have to learn and trust that the best and most effective way to be safe from these destructive forces is to avoid having the very first experience of using them, since if they do, they may fall deeper and deeper into a trap from which, in the majority of cases, they may never be able to free themselves later in life. The other attraction, when used within a wisely committed covenant, can be one of the most pleasing and delicious ingredients of life. However, when incorrectly indulged in, may work as a dangerous poison, with detrimental effects on both mind and body. This is the physiological attraction to and relationship with a person of the opposite gender.

Teaching our youth the subject of how to indulge in sex and related matters correctly and wisely in their lives is not as easy as showing them how to swim in water. To learn to play with water safely, they just need to practice and try to perfect the technique of using their muscles and reflexes correctly to float on water while using less energy, at the same time paying attention to adequate rules of safety. To learn the right approach to sex, they have to study the detailed task of appropriate social behaviors, the need for genuine love in dealing with another person's emotions, and the need to practice a lot of self-restraint which may at times require much willpower and strength of faith.

The more the members of a society control their sexual desires, avoid their abuse, make use of them wisely through proper application of principles of living, with the support of faith and logic, the more they shall overcome emotional temptations, and the healthier that society can be. The wrongdoings and outcomes related to such sexual indulgence unleash the most detrimental forces, capable of decaying the foundations of any society's well-being.

From their young age, our future generations should understand the truth about sexual pleasure as a reinforcing bond of a pre-existing friendship or attachment between two people of the opposite sex. They need to learn that only after two persons have developed adequate attachment to each other with genuine friendship and have reached mutual agreement with their sound minds, should they become involved in consummation of physical pleasures with each other.

Ideally, we should be good examples to the young, showing them that we try to obey the above rule by not taking advantage of those who are not allowed to us for this purpose, even through lustful touching and other ways of gaining sexual pleasure, including the use of our words and our sight. It is equally important to teach the younger generation that the better people present themselves to the society in a modest and more decent fashion in regard to the way they dress, speak and behave, trying to keep from causing the eruption of evil temptations.

To get involved in the practice of physical sex while lacking the needed mutual affection or love is like playing with chessmen without knowing how to play the game of chess. The child or adult who plays with the chess set just as a toy, even if temporarily fascinated with the handling of it, cannot imagine the extent of the pleasure that some others gain from playing the real game with a like set. The criminal who takes sexual advantage of someone without the needed previous agreement is like the person who steals a chess set, handling it carelessly, causing it damage, yet not even having tasted the satisfaction of playing the game.

Some may look for variety, while changing repeatedly, using different sets as their toys, yet they are not getting close to appreciate the enjoyment that can be achieved through the game of chess by the ones who make proper use of the set.

A couple who have lived together for a long time with strong bilateral affection, can in their older age, obtain much more romantic and longer lasting pleasure from each other, with or without getting seriously involved in physical sex, than the ones who approach sex physically without its emotional content. The older couple, who have such a strong bonding love, can be compared to the masters of chess who may enjoy playing the game of chess with their eyes closed, without real need for the physical set.

8

To Choose What is Good for All

It is not right that in our society we develop the tendency of providing our support only to those who belong to our own groups. Instead, we should try to have a more favorable attitude towards the better persons. We have to help the ones who perform their duties more conscientiously in every way to serve the society as a whole.

If there is, for example, an election in progress to choose somebody for a position when there are a number of candidates from different groups, the members of each group strongly support their own candidate. This is done partly due to the pre-existing prejudice towards people of their own party with the same identifying quality and partly because of the expectation of possible favors towards their group, if that candidate is elected. Both of these attitudes are incorrect, as the people should elect the one who is, in their judgment, a better person, being more suitable for the position. In the same way, the elected official ought to do what is expected to be the best for the whole society, not only for the ones who were more helpful in the election.

Observation of this unselfish rule may reassure a better future for our society, improving the quality of life for all of us and for the coming generations.

9

Our Groups in Friendship

We should encourage people to attain friendship, unity, and cooperation, proceeding to form a universal society or body, functioning with greater harmony among its members. To approach this goal successfully, we must refrain from making idols and flawless heroes out of other persons, so that we do not oppose each other unwisely in their support. We should avoid excessive emphasis on an individual's importance, whether a religious leader, a political figure, the extremely wealthy, or a successful person in sports.

We ought to keep from forming groups that can be following different leaders to the point that we are manipulated into group behavior, separating us from and placing us against other wonderful people with perhaps equally good intentions. We should form groups and follow the leaders in cooperation, assisting each other for better performance towards serving the society. With this intention, the groups can help each other, as larger groups, for more successful achievements. Even on the occasions that some groups are placed as opponents to compete, such as in the games and sports, there should be no dislike among the members merely because of being on opposite teams, nor any improper hateful remarks, propaganda, or actions against each other.

To emphasize the importance of the individuals is a function some members of our news media practice, who may give wings to the person they admire, one day making an angel with wonderful qualities based on past achievements. In the same way they may let us know with presentation of evidence and documents found in places hard to imagine, what evil acts someone has committed, which person may happen to be the same one who was admired by them on another occasion.

We human beings do good and bad. We can use the actions and the qualities of other people as examples to study and to use as guidance. We may be influenced appropriately in a positive or negative manner from the rights and wrongs they have done. We may appreciate the nice character and admirable qualities of better people, receiving from them much more positive influence on our lives. Yet, we should not consider them perfect.

It is not the individual but the actions and, even at a higher level of importance, the intentions of the person that we ought to appreciate.

It is not right that we try to make pictures and statues of the people whom we honor, or have streets and places named after them. We should make less of an issue of the person and the name. We should rather learn what good that person said or did and make use of it to help us be good and do better. It is right to respect and honor properly the nobler citizens while they are among us. Once they have passed away, it is their good deeds and words of wisdom that remain to be used by the people as a valuable beacon and guide in making our journey through the hazy and complicated maze of life more pleasant and successful. In this maze we need to find the right path to the ultimate goal, keeping safely away from the many tempting distractions on the way. From the experience of the ones who have been through it already, we may learn a great deal. Yet, we should have our eyes open and our mind on guard, so that we do not follow another person's way totally, including the mistakes and wrongdoings.

On the other hand, while observing the ones who are accustomed to doing wrong, we may learn what behavior and actions we should refrain from, but if there is something good that they have done, we ought not to disregard it.

The young ones, who are to form the individual functioning cells of our future society, have to be very careful in selecting any role models. They should wisely pay attention to the sensible guidance of their loving parents and other devoted individuals. They ought to follow the path of the ones who are really serving the society rather than imitating blindly someone who has had obvious achievements, which are, in fact, useless or harmful for the continued well-being of the society.

We have to respect appropriately, pay attention to, and learn from the good that we discover in people, but we should avoid making faultless heroes out of such individuals. In this way we may be safe from formation of groups following the intentions and instructions of the persons who may abuse our efforts, leading our groups to become useless, wasted, or even harmful members of the society.

If we follow this rule of being open-minded about others, we may also avoid forming one opinion or practicing the same judgment towards all of the individuals whom we consider grouped together because of some common qualities, different from ours. In each group of people that we consider separate from another group or from our own, regardless of what characters identify them, there must exist variable degrees of human qualities. It is unwise, incorrect, and unfair to treat the whole group the same way or make comments and suggestions considering them all alike.

10

A Destructive Fire

Drinking alcohol has been known for a very long time to be detrimental to the well-being of any society. Although alcohol has many useful applications in medicine, chemistry, industry and other areas of our daily life, it has no place in the normal physiology of the human body. We should stay away from this very powerful evil in our life. There is no moderation or a sensible way of drinking alcohol, as any amount of it is too much to drink. It is with the intention of keeping it to a low limit that many who later become alcoholics approach it initially. Yet, those suffering from alcoholism are only a very small portion of its victims. The much larger population of the society, while consuming alcohol in volumes which are, in their poisoned thinking, moderation, are hurt healthwise as well as socially and in their family life. Also, a great number are injured in different ways, physically and emotionally, by others who drink.

If alcohol has any claimed benefit for the body, the benefit withstands no value against the magnitude of its harm and destructive force. In the same way that it causes fatal illness in individuals, it can produce serious disruptions in the whole society. When a house is on fire, the benefit obtained from the heat of the fire on a cold winter night or the magnificent scene for the viewers, is obviously negligible, compared to the great loss of the house and its contents. In the same way, alcoholic beverages burn societies, and so many of us are, sadly, fascinated by viewing the destruction!!

11

The Outlook for the Future

Observing the young ones of our society and the way many of them are living can make us very concerned and at times quite worried about our future generations or the future of our generation. One can see among them, the behavior of a possible smaller minority of precious jewels who are our valuable investments for a later society. I do not see the need to write much about them except to mention that we ought to thank God for their being here, as they are for us a source of satisfaction for the present and hope for the future. I would like, however, to write a few paragraphs for the young ones who have the capability or tendency of striving towards perfection but, due to some misguiding influences, have been diverted from that path.

At any stage in our life, whether as a baby in the cradle, a young adolescent at school, the grown-up working at home or outside, or the elderly in retirement, we are looking for means of gaining pleasure. This may be reached in different ways. It may be the result of the interruption of a physical or emotional discomfort, the satisfaction of a physiologic requirement, the mental contentment due to an achievement, or meeting of some desired circumstances. Whatever is causing our joy, we are consciously and subconsciously concerned about how fulfilling it is and how long-lasting. We are blessed with an innumerable variety of pleasures in our lives, so what really matters is not one single pleasure at a moment but the collective value of the pleasures or the final result after balancing them against each other. There are often situations that we need to sacrifice one pleasure for the sake of another which is more pleasing or longer lasting.

A baby may drop a toy when presented with another one. The hungry may tolerate difficulties to reach a tasty dish. The comfortable bed may be left easily, interrupting the sweet sleep, for meeting a very dear person, and the preparations for traveling are tolerated happily for reaching a desired destination. The balancing of the pleasures, exchanging them or evaluating them against each other, is done by all of us.

There are some among our young ones who have a broader view in this calculation, realizing that longer lasting future happiness is preferable, so they sacrifice, when need be, some transient pleasures of the moment. While generatihg better possible pleasure for their future, this group can also taste, at that moment, the joy of satisfaction of having performed as they feel they should have. There are other young individuals who are behaving as if they are living only for the moment. When considering their attitude towards the society and towards their own life and its long–range future, it appears as if they have been made to wear some wrong kind of glasses which make them both nearsighted and with a narrow field of vision. They seem to observe only the very near future with clarity, leaving the vast area of the faraway portion of the future of their own life as a fuzzy view, without even showing enough interest or courage in trying to make it look better later as they get closer to it. Even with regard to the present moments of their life, they are but paying attention to only limited aspects of possibilities, leaving some valuable facts of life out of their visual field.

While looking for joy, happiness, pleasure, or whatever they may call it, they do not realize that they are blinded from seeing many important points, and as a result, making grave mistakes that can adversely affect their later happiness. Instead of following the advice of their parents or their other benevolent elders and paying attention to learn the proper manners for becoming decent grown-ups of the future, they follow the recommendations of misguided peers. They adopt, under the influence of a wrongly selected group of friends, an unpleasant behavior. They do this instead of studying with enthusiasm in the search of how to become productive individuals, supplying the society, in due time, with the right service and their own family or other dear ones with needed securities. They engage themselves in time-wasting social gatherings which are accompanied by activities that can cause harm to self and to others. I sincerely encourage them to remove those blurring glasses in order to obtain a better picture of their life and to see their own future more clearly. If we pay enough attention to the future, we may learn to enjoy our moments while trying to be better, performing more correctly, and doing what is needed to ensure more possible happiness for a later time. We may then easily sacrifice any temporary pleasures, and more definitely that which is not right, for the sake of storing more joy for our future. After all, we can see clearly that at any moment our degree of happiness in a similar circumstance is very much affected by our view of future, if we look at it carefully or have adequate concern about it.

Consider, for example, the degree of a student's happiness during a similar lecture on two different occasions: at one time with plans to go to a desired place with the family or friends after the lecture and at another time expecting difficulties after the session because of having lost or damaged some valuable item. While listening to the same kind of discussion with the same teacher, the degree of enjoying that same lecture can be quite different, depending on what is expected to follow. Think of how much two people enjoy their meal when one of them expects to be promoted at work on the following day to a well-desired status, the other one having received the notice of losing an employment. The degree of enjoying the same kind of food at the same place of service can be very different, depending on how the future is expected to be. Our younger generation should pay attention to the fact that these kinds of examples apply to all of the aspects of our actions in this life and the outlook of our long-range future.

Our youth who are, by way of enjoying their time, consumed by harmful habits, should spend some useful effort to change their ways. When they become accustomed to right thoughts and deeds and look ahead to their distant future with optimism, they may taste, at any moment of their present time, more of a real pleasure mixed with satisfaction. They may then enjoy studying with greater courage, as they know that with a better education it is more likely that they find a career of their choice in which they perform better and enjoy what they do. Once they get used to doing what is right for the future and of benefit to the society, using their efforts to proceed and do well, they can be pleased with advancing in the correct direction. They may then look with a critical view to their own injured past and to the ongoing mistakes of some peers who are spending their moments doing what is pure waste of time, such as some of their social gatherings or many of their current unhealthy entertainments; or what can hurt their health and future, such as the use of alcoholic beverages, cigarettes or other addictive substances; or what is ethically and morally inappropriate, such as promiscuity; or what is harmful to the whole society, such as all of what has been mentioned above as well as many other wrongdoings which finally, directly or indirectly, affect the well-being and future health of our society.

The more these courageous young individuals of our society notice the mistakes of their peers, while trying to correct them rather than being affected under their pressure, the more rewarding pleasure they can sense, with more perception of encouragement for further progress in that right path. Then they can see not only a clearer picture of their future but also a broader view of the present life, realizing that each moment is filled with a variety of responsibilities towards not only themselves but others and the society as a whole. These responsibilities can make their social life more pleasant when they are fulfilled through the mutual cooperation of the members of the society in the same way that a family's efforts to take care of the problems of each other and the group can be accompanied by much pleasure.

It is wise to pay attention to the fact that the level of the pleasure gained from what we do, or what we have, can vary to a great extent depending on our expectations, or what we are used to. At any given time, while having proper ambition for improvement, we may be happier remembering that there are many who wish to be in the circumstance that we are in, or we may increase our discontent if we keep wishfully thinking of the better possibilities out of our reach. Our young ones can try to learn how to enjoy the time that they spend in being good, just with the great satisfaction gained from having controlled their selfish and temporary pleasures for the sake of joy of future and happiness of all concerned.

Perhaps we, as the grown-up members of society, carry some blame for the bad influences on our young ones. The variety of wrongdoings observed in our society cannot be without continuous ill-effect on the life of our younger generation. This will continue unless we correct the three places that influence the education of our children, namely the home, the school and the general society. At home, the serious problems of family life can affect the young mind from very early times with possibly some irreversible damage. Also, we cannot seriously expect the children of our society to keep from doing the mistakes that the parents are accustomed to doing at home or in the society. If I expect my child not to tell a lie, I should myself avoid lying. At school, we have to provide the best possible education for our children, with teachers who are compensated as well as they deserve and who are suitable for such an important responsibility. The society in general, including the areas of news media, entertainment, and many other fields, some of which are mentioned elsewhere in this book, plus the behavior of us as the adults, should be cleansed from imperfection as much as possible if we really want to reduce, as well as we can, our society's harmful influences on the sensitive minds of our young ones.

If we leave the young ones of the opposite gender without proper and modest outfits together in the classrooms or without adequate guidance or supervision during other activities, we are guilty of promoting the confusion of their delicate feelings, resulting in a chain of serious events destroying their future happiness and our society's prosperity.

Another negative influence in our society on the younger minds is the idea of old age, giving them the impression that old age is synonymous with misery, illness, loneliness, incapacity and desertion. Some of our old ones keep complaining about a variety of problems, with the whole society insisting on the incorrect notion that every old person must be missing his or her youth and wishing to have been able to go back to it. As the expectation of future directly affects the degree of our happiness in life, the above–mentioned, self-generated problem of our society can cause some degree of inherent subconscious sadness or basic depression in the mind of anyone. As a result, many young ones, feeling incorrectly hopeless about their distant future, may conclude wrongly that they better enjoy their time while they can. Through this approach, not only do they destroy so much of their hopes for the future, but also they can cause possible permanent mental and physical harm to themselves and to others. This attitude can, in turn, produce misery in their old age, and as a result we may have the vicious cycle continue to destroy the image of old age and the health of the young mind.

Instead, how wonderful it would be if we show clearly that dedicated young ones can, through proper attitude towards life, by owning their responsibilities correctly, perhaps enjoy years of productive life, and reach old age, which, depending on our expectations, may be enjoyed at least as much as any other period of life. At that higher extreme of life, one may be content more and more with achievements rather than plans, with successes rather than efforts, and with the happiness seen in the dear ones and the society rather than personal enjoyments. This, to the right mind, can be much more pleasing in the same way that the parents may not enjoy eating a delicious food as much as they enjoy watching their children eating it. Above all, since the confidence towards the future can have much effect on the pleasure of a moment, if the old person has tried to save adequately for the everlasting hereafter, the true joy in that person's mind cannot be compared to any other worldly happiness. The youth who live wisely may pass through the different periods of life with an adequate supply of pleasure, possibly having an abundance of joy in their old age. For those individuals, the final stage of this life is just the pleasant end of the beginning.

12

Misplaced Securities

I do not know if the majority of our people feel a proper sense of security:
- The security of having adequate control over their own belongings.
- The security that if they do not bother others, they won't be bothered unfairly by others.
- The security that if they are trying to serve the society in an honest productive manner will cause them to have a continuous supply of whatever comfort they deserve.
- The security of being able to keep their principles in accordance with ethical, moral, or other standards without corruptive influences disturbing their peace of mind or the decent lives of the ones close to them.
- The security that they do not have to tolerate a variety of inconveniences in their daily lives due to other people's dishonesty at different levels, with abuse of the resources of the society.
- The security that when they try very hard not to have any prejudice towards others, nobody will treat them unfairly just because of minor differences that may exist between them.
- The security that if they are in an authorized place of stay, no matter how crowded or deserted, at whatever time of the day or night, nobody will take advantage of them or of what belongs to them.
- The security that in the various stages of their progress in society, and their being successful with projects or other achievements for reaching their goals in any career, they can rely on the quality of their performance or product

rather than expectation of wrongdoings to satisfy somebody's financial or other ambitions.

- The security that when they present their problems to responsible professionals, whether the police, the dentist, the lawyer, the surgeon or the car mechanic, they can expect to have their confidence satisfied, and the professionals performing their tasks as they expect others to perform for them.
- The security that when they make some investment, trusting in somebody or some organization, they will not be cheated with people disappearing illegally or the investment vanishing in an unfair manner legally through bankruptcy or other techniques.
- The security that if they are victims of minor or major crimes, the criminals, if caught, receive adequate punishment without undue delay.
- The security that if they are bothered by someone who is stronger, whether a physically more muscular individual on the street or a person with higher influence elsewhere, the bystanders or the whole powerful society offer their timely support, rather than being afraid of their own involvement with the stronger person.

I do not know whether the probability exists, when dealing with more than trivial matters in small communities, that those responsible for the exercise of law, order, and justice would be taking the side of ordinary citizens who are oppressed but brave enough to confront the powerful, or the side of those who manipulate them because they have strong political, legal, or financial influence. Nor can I guess the extent of similar possibilities, of course, at a higher scale of involvement, in the larger communities, and in other levels of our society.

Those who use their worldly influence in the wrong way, taking advantage of the innocence of society, are making a grave mistake. They feel that through their financial or other power they can manipulate others of small or large numbers to follow their wishes at all times. They have the notion that through this attitude they may be able to control the groups of people, almost as slaves, working harder for the security and comfort of the few under their own protection. They are so blinded by the sparkling of their gold that they cannot appreciate the direction of true light. They like to go towards temporary illumination, like the flies going to the candle light, not realizing that when they are too close they can get burned. They do not understand that the power and treasures of this world are truly valuable only if used correctly; otherwise they can be the cause of trouble. Through their limited vision, concentrated on their worldly assets, they cannot clearly discern the truth:

- The truth that they are not going to take with them their power, but only the result of how they have used it in this world. If they have not used it as they should to store appropriately for the hereafter, they shall continuously fear the moment of their leaving it behind, rather than enjoying their life when looking to the future with much hope for the profit from what they have saved through their actions.

- The truth that while they are all the time approaching the departure from their luxuries of this world with a continuous subconscious fear or worry for a hopeless distant future, those who are spending those luxuries right are enjoying this life, with passage of time, looking with hopes towards their ultimate destination.

- The truth that in the process of collecting and safeguarding what they can get of money and power they are suffering from continuous stress. They cannot enjoy the luxuries that they have when they get used to them, any more than the average people are pleased with what they are accustomed to; to sustain the supply of that luxury much effort has to be spent continuously. They may often wish they could live an average, comfortable life away from their problems, but they find no easy way out. They are stressed in spite of luxury, yet they feel insecure without it.

- The truth that in spite of their efforts they cannot guarantee long-standing happiness for their close ones, who may suffer from the consequences of corruption brought by the wealth they have but without proper discipline in spending it.

- The truth that through their self-centered concerns, rather than spending their efforts towards the improvement of the living conditions of the majority and the whole society, they are not helping but hurting the future of the world as a whole, and hurting the people of the future, including their own distant future generations and the descendants of their dear ones.

When they abuse their power, they can cause more and more sadness among others, generating more hatred, dragging their own few people with them into the stressful world of being disliked by the majority rather than helping them feel the happiness of living in an atmosphere of unselfish sacrifice surrounded by a spirit of friendship with the whole society and cooperation of all people.

There are, at the same time, so many others with an abundance of wealth or influence in this world, who are spending it wisely by performing the right service for their people and the whole society. They are satisfied both from having it and using it in the correct way. They try to help in preparing a better life for all mankind.

We may affect the future of life on this planet through our actions. If the coming generations learn to be overly money-conscious and greedy, they shall live in misery. Each person tries hard to devise clever ways for becoming richer and richer, without sharing any part of the wealth with the others; for one family's false sense of security many others could be left deprived of their basic necessities. This would be a society made of individuals who sacrifice the comfort of others for their own financial gains, increasing the level of stress for all. The ones who will be wealthy but selfish shall continue to struggle with their stressful lives, while their guilty consciences and their insecurities shall cause their partial seclusion. Those who are relatively poor or oppressed, dealing with magnitudes of problems, may have been the children of the rich ones of the past.

If the future people of this world wisely cooperate, while trying to live as a large family on earth with mutual friendship, each sacrificing pleasures of self to increase the comfort of the others, without discriminating according to racial or other unimportant differences, they may reach the point of having profound joy when sharing true pleasure with everyone. This can be a great feeling when all are happy and each of them is getting an increase of pleasure from observing the others' satisfaction and joy. That would be a society of individuals who try to be good, live well, and do right.

13

The True Pleasures

We can enjoy what we are doing, whenever it is being done for the sake of somebody or something that we like very much. If we really like our car, we may clean it with pleasure. When we are truly happy with our work or some project that we are trying to accomplish at every step of the way, in doing what is related to it, we are eager to proceed tirelessly while enjoying our efforts towards the achievements. If we are assembling a toy for a child whom we love very much, or we are repairing some object for our beloved parents, or doing something nice for someone we are fond of, we may do it with so much pleasure that not only do we not feel tired, but we may even forget or ignore some of our physiologic needs, such as becoming hungry and eating our meal, or feeling sleepy at our usual bedtime. This can all happen when we truly like something that we do or someone that we do it for.

Is it then possible to imagine how much we may enjoy our life if we devote our deeds for the love of The Supreme Being? Then perhaps we would enjoy every moment of our life to the point that the most difficult times can be tolerated with ease, and any possible pain may be ameliorated with the effect of this most powerful spiritual remedy. In such a life we might expect our passage through every corner of this maze to be joyous, satisfying, and much more purposeful.

14

The Judgments

In the delivery of proper justice, punishment is neither retaliation nor revenge towards the criminal, but a necessary lesson for educating the society. Offering sympathy to the criminal, trying to abate or avoid the appropriate penalty, is unfairness towards the innocents and the whole society. To keep the society as free from crime as possible, the punishment of the criminals must be adequately severe, carried out without undue delay, and properly evident to the public. Remember that our insisting on the rights of the criminal and trying to find excuses to avoid timely and appropriate punishment are almost all results of our emotional feelings, mixed with sympathy or fear, rather than logic. Even if we were worried and concerned about our own future or the future of our dear ones, that one of us might someday receive such a punishment after a wrongdoing or by mistake, this concern would be, obviously, sentimental and not based on sound reasoning.

While enforcing justice with the criminal, the society is neither presenting any hate nor making a judgment on the quality of that person. Whether that criminal, deep inside, is much better or worse a person than we imagine, the severity of the punishment is according to the committed crime and not depending on our sentimental perceptions. Our religious instructions have ordained adequately severe punishment for the criminals, but we the people, by letting our personal emotions interfere with our adequate reasoning, refrain from carrying out the proper order because of a multitude of factors influencing our attitude with regard to criminal justice.

Forgiveness is a wonderful quality when practiced by the victims of crime, but not by the judiciary system in the process of trial and punishment of the criminal. If I decided to forgive, deep in my heart, the person who robbed my wallet, feeling sorry for that individual's poverty in finance, wisdom, and faith, this may be an admirable behavior. On the other hand, when the widow of a murdered husband and her children have not forgiven and are desperately asking for severe punishment of the murderer, we ought to be fair to them by practicing applicable justice. If I, as a member of the jury, let the excuse of forgiving, or my personal fear of the blame of having caused another person's death, or my reasoning that unless seen with my own eyes I can never have absolute certainty about that crime, or the feeling that I would like to be considered by others as a kind and softhearted rather than a rough person, interfere with the carrying out of my due responsibility, and as a result vote against the killing of the murderer, this is purely a selfish attitude. In this case, perhaps I am so involved with my personal feelings that I don't pay attention to my participation in the wrongdoing, becoming indirectly an encouragement to the present crime and perhaps an accessory to the future crimes committed by this criminal and by many others who might reach a negative conclusion and draw an inappropriate lesson from this trial.

In the exercise of proper justice, the criminal's rights should be perhaps observed in the same way as the criminal observed the victim's rights at the time of the crime. This is the price the criminal pays for the committed crime and is not in any way society's fault. It is also possibly quite fair if what was done by the criminal to the victim, is done as closely as possible or practical, by law to the criminal. While controlling our personal feelings, being very logical, unselfish, and unemotional, we may help our society tremendously by fairer and more adequate exercise of justice in support of our innocent community. We can practice severe physical punishments which would obviously be more effective than prison terms and less of a burden to the society. The robbers and habitual thieves can receive severe physical punishment, the rapists can become disabled, and the murderers put to death, as they deserve.

In removing from a patient that part of the body, that bears a life-threatening disease, we cannot let our emotional reasoning interfere with the performance of the procedure. The expert, such as a knowledgeable surgeon, with logical considerations, should make the decision and, when indicated, carry out the operation. It is not for the sympathetic or sentimental friends and relatives to perform such a vigorous act. The operation may seem to be harsh and cruel to the unaccustomed eye, yet it is done to save the person's health. If we are dealing with a patient who has a gangrenous gallbladder, instead of the rights of the biliary tract including the gallbladder, we should be concerned about the rights of that person as a whole and carry out the operation of removal of the gallbladder before the patient dies altogether with the whole biliary system.

It is very clear that if emotional and selfish arguments are excluded, the physical punishments of the criminals must be practiced vigorously by the professionals of the system of justice to protect the health of the society and to help in providing for the innocent people the security that they deserve to have. This is both an appropriate justice and a good lesson to any potential criminal; this is not cruelty. A true cruelty is forgiving such criminals through insanity or other excuses, exposing vast numbers of innocent individuals to their crimes in the future. The sentences should be carried out as harshly as they are supposed to be, yet without our showing any personal hate. The death sentence is to let the society observe that the one who murders an innocent person suffers a death. Lethal injections of sedative or anesthetic drugs cause easy and comfortable death, which is not what the murderer deserves. It gives the appearance of our assisting the murderer in a gentle way to commit suicide.

Instead of our guiding everybody's sympathy with the encouragement received from the news media, the writers of books, and the movie producers towards occasional innocents who have or may become victims of mistaken judgment and punishment, we should pay attention to the vast number of real criminals who manage to be protected from proper punishment.

We, as members of the society, ought to be concerned with the protection of human rights in the world in its real sense. How could our conscience permit us to close our eyes from seeing the rights of the whole society of innocent people, but to keep them open to see the rights of the criminals? How could we call this human rights protection when it is clear that the rights of these two groups are in conflict and clash with each other? One group being the innocents, who could be potential prey in the future and the other group the leopards of the society, who are the actual predators. They are truly not the pussycats that we observe during the trials and in the courtrooms.

We must punish adequately those who are believed to have abused their freedom and have committed the crimes so that the severe punishments are noticed, making a very loud noise, keeping a large number of potential and criminal stalkers of society tamed and under control.

To spend too much time, from the moment the suspect is in custody until the sentence is carried out, can cause tremendous loss of a society's resources. It also nullifies one of the main purposes of the trial, which is the proper education of the whole society. While taking much time for the trial, scheduling the many trivial discussions about the validity of the evidence according to legal loopholes, the sanity of the criminal, or the effect of the suspect's distant past memories on the present crime, while spending long periods of argument on how reasonable is our certainty about the criminal's guilt and while guarding the one who continues unnecessarily to wait for the already decided sentence to be carried out possibly after years of waiting, we are wasting people's time and society's money, both of which could be better used elsewhere. Even the ones who are earning or have financial interest through these lengthy processes may use their time in another productive capacity in the society.

It is the speedy trial, with just the necessary discussions to present proper evidence and adequate defense, reaching a decision with reasonable certainty resulting, when indicated, in swift and severe punishment of the criminals, that can be an adequate deterrent, while saving future potential victims.

Not practicing aggressive justice towards the criminals is unfair, not only to the victims of the crimes and the innocent society as the future sufferers, but also towards the other potential criminals of our society who could in proper circumstances live a fairly normal life. Instead, such persons, having observed the gentleness of justice, may become careless about the rights of others, spending the rest of their precious lives astray, probably in misery with related problems and possibly, for part of it, in jail.

All criminals are not bad individuals. We should have a community that seriously discourages its members from committing crime of any kind, at whatever level or class of our society.

When there is reasonable certainty of the guilt of the criminal, this in itself should be enough for justice to be practiced and the sentence to be carried out. Our minor doubts are not to cause hesitancy in our decisions.

If in the process of trial and conviction of one hundred murderers we have included, for example, five or ten innocent individuals who are killed by mistake, this is very acceptable to any sound judgment when we consider the fact that to save the unknown possible ten we let the other ninety live, ultimately to succeed in killing hundreds more innocent people. Besides, through this vicious act of sympathy we are giving a wrong message to the society. As a result, much larger numbers of potential criminals may kill and harm many other innocent people.

So much can be happening, so many may be killed and hurt because of our trying to save such a small number. In other words, it requires the sacrifice of life, safety, and comfort of a vast number of our people to satisfy, in a selfish manner, our own conscience, just to show off that we are saving rather than harming, no matter how unreasonably or what the society would have to pay for the price.

It is also of utmost importance that with the process of trial and its consequences, adequate measures of safety and permanent immunity should be observed for those involved in the exercise of justice against any possible legal, physical, or other harm by potential criminals or their agents. On the other hand, inappropriate actions in the process, such as lying with malice when called as a witness or abuse of official authority in framing an innocent with guilt, would be cause for receiving much more severe punishment than for ordinary crimes.

What I wrote in the last few paragraphs may hopefully encourage some of the people who have a fixed attitude of sympathy towards criminals, who call it human rights, instead of criminal and crime protection, to put aside for once their sentiments and pay attention to the said reasoning with a more logical understanding. Perhaps by looking through this new window, which they had previously resisted opening their mind to, they will see a different and much more sensible view of our world of justice and dealing with crime and criminals.

We cannot judge with certainty the quality of a person through the observation of that person's acts, even if it is the commitment of a crime. We only judge the person's guilt in a crime with reasonable certainty, then the punishment is mainly for the education of the others, in trying to provide the needed atmosphere of safety and comfort for the innocent society as a whole.

15

Desires, Tamed or Untamed

When listening to the discussions about the problems of our society, in relation to sex, many of those involved in the discussions, including some of the parents, are missing the most important points. They debate on the subjects of teenage pregnancy, abortion, and sexually transmitted diseases. It seems many of them do not have real objection to their children's involvement in promiscuity; they are only concerned about the immediate problems or health hazards.

Many of these adults claim to be religious, in some way believing in God. If they themselves are refraining from sexual misbehaviors, yet according to whatever religious group they belong to, it is obviously wrong to condone the uncontrolled freedom of their children and the other young ones of society to the point that they are engaged in an undisciplined, irresponsible sexual friendship or relationship. We human beings are supposed to be more understanding, more civilized, and more capable of controlling our emotions and desires compared to animals. Even some animals have a proper discipline for their courtship.

Since the attraction between the persons of opposite gender is the strongest of temptations in this world, we need strong dedication, with team effort, to help our younger generation have a better possibility of passage through their wonderful period of puberty on the right path, without being distracted by the pull of this powerful desire, which may entrap them, resulting in physical and mental injuries that can affect their future adversely, making them disabled during their journey through precious years of life.

The young should learn from the older generation, both by following their advice and emulating them as practical examples in order to control and guide their desires at every moment correctly, following appropriate principles in the interest of their own future and a better future for the society as a whole. We are responsible for carrying out the challenging but rewarding task of teaching our adolescents the truth, letting them know the important facts related to this complex and at times complicated subject. To let them know that, like almost everything else in this life, if they control their desires when dealing with sex, at any time avoiding its unwise or improper utilization, they may save for themselves the opportunity of enjoying it much more in the future. If, to the contrary, they let their reinless wild horse of temptations be in control, taking them off the right path, they may, following transient moments of pleasure, suffer from untoward, long-lasting consequences. It is not only the contraction of some serious diseases that should matter, with their terrible complications, or an undesired pregnancy that can complicate their future. Many young ones have aged quickly with depression and other problems as a result of misguided sex, to the point that they could never experience the taste of a decent adult life.

The young who control their sexual desire correctly may enjoy it much more when they reach the right time of partnership with due responsibilities in accordance with their faith and the laws of the society. To succeed in doing so, they may need a lot of support and advice from their parents and other responsible elders. Then, as they have not become corrupted in this aspect of their life, nor accustomed to let themselves freely be attracted to others inadvertently, they and their partner may continue to enjoy mutually the relationship that is lawfully theirs. When they are used to self-restraint, avoiding improper sexual pleasure from others, and refraining from the abuse of their sight, words, or touch in a lustful manner towards those not meant to be for them, they may enjoy their correct relationship much more fully, with long-lasting pleasure and sense of satisfaction. They may continue to enjoy the emotional aspects of it into their old age, even if the related physical capabilities may diminish.

Those who have abused their sexual desires without proper self-control find themselves in need of greater variety in order to be able to gain their short-lasting pleasures, yet mixed with feelings of guilt. They have a sense of insecurity about their future. They cannot continue to enjoy only what is their own for very long. Thence, the frequency of their separations from each other, after short acquaintances, results in social, psychological, emotional, and other complications for our society. This attitude among the young ones of our society may cause severe emotional sequelae for some of them, destroying their future happiness.

Perhaps we can compare the attitude of the ones mentioned in the last paragraph to alcoholics. They let themselves freely use what they should not, taking advantage of what is in their reach, against correct ethical, religious, or social principles. With continuation of this attitude of abuse, many side effects are seen for these individuals and the whole society. There is also a gradual rise in the threshold for their gaining any of the apparent pleasures, so they may get more and more involved with their wrongdoing while having less satisfaction, yet finding no easy way out of it towards a normal happy life. They use the moment to please their desires while they do not dare to look to their distant future of old age since with what they are storing for it, they are hopelessly afraid of its arrival.

Together with these misconducts, comes the whole range of serious problems involving their children as the future generation of our society, many of whom do not see much of a family life, or at least not a happy one.

In the process of searching for their undisciplined transient sexual pleasures, some of the promiscuous individuals, while lacking proper moral and religious ethics to limit their activities, may become affected by seriously diverted behaviors, generating for themselves physical and mental miseries, and for their society a variety of social, moral, and other problems.

16

Causation of
Dislike and Distrust

It is nice to see friendship, peace and trust among the people. There are many who encourage this kind of attitude in the society. There are also some who, even if claiming the contrary, promote disturbed relationships and hate between others for their own potential gains. As an example, some of the influential members of three groups of people may be mentioned, who present this behavior although there may be only a small minority in each group.

Large numbers of those who practice law are engaged in the protection of the innocent against the wicked, the support of the weak in front of the aggressor, and the prevention or dissolution of a variety of problems our society can be dealing with on a daily basis. They correctly make the ones at fault pay compensation for the damages they have caused. There are also some who generate problems or magnify the existing ones. They encourage individuals or groups to file unfair claims of enormous magnitude against each other. They promote hatred instead of forgiveness. They present true or false damages and faults, blown out of proportion, trying to extract as much money as possible from guilty or innocent, from rich or poor or, as they proudly claim, from the insurance companies, indirectly making all of us pay for it, so that they can add to their wealth through the priceless injury they cause to the society. They may not worry about their client's opponent losing a job or house or perhaps the security of future life, as long as they earn some personal profit in finance and reputation.

Another group to be mentioned are some of the people with authority in the production of what is known to us as the mass media. Many responsible individuals, through the extremely effective network of radio, television, cinema, books, magazines, or other publications and means of public communication educate us continuously, offering vast amounts of beneficial knowledge to our society. There are others, however, who try to produce whatever sells more favorably, to attract large numbers of people, inconsiderate of their potential damage to our society and its future. Among many other detrimental effects that their productions have, they also promote dislike between groups of people. They undermine the trust that should exist between friends and family members; the confidence that is needed between client and the professional, the public and the police, the employee and the employer, the customer and the owner of business; the respect that is expected between the parents and their children, and teachers and their students. They cause hate between groups of people when they present problems that exist due to racial, political, religious, cultural or other reasons, with exaggeration, enraging those involved. They selfishly feel that the showing of the fights and the wrongdoings is attractive for their business, though resulting in further violence, with people hurting each other more.

The other group involves those who are engaged in international politics. Among the members of the governments of different countries and involved politicians, there are many who are struggling, with trust in God, to prepare a better future political world. They work hard to promote true democracy and peace among the nations of this planet. They may get involved in wars bravely in defense against the aggressors. There are also some who make nations hate and hurt each other without good reason. They may cause battles and wars in the name of peace or may actually oppress people in the name of democracy. They may get vast numbers of friends and enemies killed with malice in the effort to keep their own prestige and position or to satisfy those in charge and the ones who put them in charge.

In each country, through an invisible cooperation between some of the people with more political influence and some of the staff of the news media, a continuous effort seems to exist to generate and increase prejudice in their own nation against other peoples of the world. To gain more power and popularity in the country, they praise their own people, compared to the other nations, making them feel they have superior qualities or that the others are taking advantage of them in some way.

Instead of letting them learn the truth, that we people in different parts of the world are basically the same, having a wide range of qualities, they make their people believe that they either have some higher qualities compared to others or that others are causing their problems or even that some are the source of potential danger to their future.

Through this kind of propaganda, instead of increasing friendship and cooperation among the inhabitants of this planet, they sustain an incorrect feeling of distrust in their people against other nations, possibly in different degrees against selected groups. They plant the seed of enmity in the hearts of their people against the masses of other wonderful nations to satisfy small favored groups. They may cause misery for many, including large numbers of people of their own country, to secure power and wealth for a few although the abundance of these worldly assets often comes with increased stress for them and may be accompanied by decay of human values. At times, they cause a change in these emotions, making friends into enemies or past enemies into friends of the future. Other times, they may keep a persistent disturbed feeling towards some particular group, to the point that some of their people may truly hate that nation as a whole.

When this attitude is observed among the other groups as well, it is very possible that two nations are placed against each other, their feelings having been manipulated by small groups of selfish individuals. As a result many good people, who could potentially be sincere friends, may hurt each other. If one country interferes with malice in the affairs of another nation without good reason, or some people of one nation feel they can do any harm to other innocent people for their own security, this attitude can be compared to the causing of injury and harm by a criminal to the victim in a selfish and inconsiderate manner. Countries and nations could be compared to individuals or persons. Through friendship, cooperation, and unselfish help, immense mutual benefits can be enjoyed by all.

17

Invisible

While each of us has, deep inside, a clear feeling of self, how can some people, just because of not finding it as a detectable part of our anatomy, deny that we have a soul? The soul is the real person or the entity that continues to exist with the capacity or ability of having feelings even after being dissociated from the material body that ceases to function as a unit. And how can some, in similar way, disbelieve in the creation of all of us and this world by The Supreme Being only because they cannot see The Creator with their eyes?

The people who believe only in the material world should remember that they cannot deny the existence of everything that is not detectable by their senses. Our capability of feeling and seeing is very limited, even towards what exists in this material world of ours. We know there are sound waves that we don't hear and light beams that we do not see.

Of all that our senses are capable of perceiving, we appreciate only the changes; otherwise, if what exists does not change in our view or feeling, we are so used to it that we do not feel its presence. For example, we do not see, under normal circumstances, the vessels inside our own eye although they are very close in front of our retina. This is because we are used to their constant image. Nor do we feel in each area of our body our skin, but what touches the skin. We do not feel the presence of our liver and so many other organs in their locations, nor every function of our stomach and intestine. We do not feel the vast magnitude of biochemical phenomena continually occurring in our systems. We do not feel so many radiations or radio waves penetrating our body at every moment. We cannot see or feel the invisible force that attracts or expels the magnets, but we understand that it is there and functioning. We do not feel the atmospheric pressure that the air exerts on our body continuously, nor do we feel the presence of the air around us, except changes and movements. We appreciate the affinity that exists between every particle of our planet, including ourselves, with the particles of so many other faraway planets or stars, but we do not expect to see any attachments.

Those who believe only in the material world accept the existence of so much which they cannot feel, through reasoning or observing the evidence of their existence. They appreciate the presence of radioactivity when depicted by a radiation counter. Then how could they not believe with certainty in The Supreme Being when every object or every function in our world is proof of the existence of The Creator?

Is it possible that our soul has the capacity for other feelings and understandings that we do not experience in this world or life? Could we possibly sense, at times, a different feeling even during this life, when asleep? Then, when we wake up, perhaps we do not remember it because we cannot feel that way when we are awake, nor do we have the ability to appreciate those feelings in our present memory with its very limited capacity.

●   .·

18

Trapped in Vicious Circles

We know that the future is very important for us. Even when we are doing, by mistake or perhaps for temporary pleasures, what may hurt our future, we feel that logically we must persist in making efforts to secure a satisfactory future. This rule is for us, as individuals, as groups, as nations, and above all as the society of mankind on earth. As the individual members of this large society, we ought to cooperate with one another in doing what may increase the chances for having a better future for all of us. The society, in turn, should effectively encourage each one of us to do what is expected to improve the possibility of a better future for all and strongly discourage everyone from doing what is logically expected to hurt the society's future.

To achieve the above-mentioned reasonable goal, we may need to force ourselves to adopt, as individuals as well as groups, the correct attitude towards the other members of the society, perhaps often going against our emotional reflexes or desires and in contrast to what many others may wrongly favor. We have to observe with an open mind the actions of the other members of our society, then logically develop a policy of how to treat the ones who deserve our respect and support, helping them so that they have a better chance of doing their good for the society. While those who carelessly or for their own selfish gains are doing what, according to our sound reasoning, can hurt the future of the society, should be treated with appropriate criticism in a manner that strongly discourages them from their wrongdoing and keeps others from adopting similar harmful acts or behavior.

The things we do that can help or hurt the future of our world are almost countless. Some of the social problems that we have possess the capability of self-reinforcement, and unless they are properly controlled before it is too late, these problems have an enhancing effect on each other, gaining momentum and becoming stronger when they are present together. These then form separate or combined vicious circles, with our society gradually entrapped in these circles and dragged towards self-destruction.

To elaborate on this issue, please let me give some examples of how, according to my personal reasoning or present feelings, we are doing or we should be doing in our society in relation to a few of the above-mentioned problems.

The subject of **sexual attraction** is one of the strongest factors that, if not controlled by proper guidelines, can cause a vicious circle with very serious destructive effects on any nation or society. With its potent influence especially on the minds of our youth, at a period in life when they are to concentrate their attention on building the foundations of their whole life and career, the distraction caused by sexual desires, with detrimental complications resulting from its incorrect application, can effectively ruin their precious future. This, I dare to say, in the present life of our society appears to be one of the worst vicious circles that we are faced with and are entrapped within.

The more irresponsible freedom we allow the members of our society in gaining lustful pleasure in a variety of ways from others, the more intoxication of the minds we may see in our society, to the point that the temporary evil sexual pleasures replace the elements of faith, wisdom, and logical principles for adequate self-restraint. As a result, those who have been poisoned in this way and become accustomed to their wrongdoing, having impaired the proper functioning of their logic, behave like the persons who are under the effects of alcohol or other drugs, encouraging the whole innocent society to adapt to their indecencies. They can sabotage the proper education of the younger generation, possibly diverting many of them from the right path, as we may easily follow the devil's way when lacking proper guidance.

There can be, in this way, escalation of the degree of our society's moral deterioration with this epidemic to the point that we become a group so affected by the sickness that we cannot fight it any more. The more misguided the young ones are with freedom to abuse their sexual desires, the more corrupted their society can become when they grow up in it. Then comes more distortion of the atmosphere of education, accordingly, for the younger ones who follow their path.

We are already feeling the effects of this vicious circle around us, and perhaps too many of us are getting used to it. Some of us condone or may encourage the young to start casual involvement with practices related to sex and romance before reaching the adequate period of life in order to become properly attached to a person of the opposite gender through serious commitments. Some of our people lack modesty, having become accustomed to exposing their bodies to the public in ways that would cause sexual temptations in others. Some use this kind of influence through much more powerful means of communication in causing moral deterioration and corruption of masses of people in our nations with their publications, means of broadcasting, or similar ways of bringing to the society words and pictures deficient in proper moral values and true modesty. Some abuse their sight, words, and touch in an unethical way, promoting sexual involvement with or obtaining lustful pleasure from others who are not allowed to them for that purpose. Against the order of the faith that they follow or that they ought to have, they indulge in sexual relationships even with those who are already committed to another person. Some present themselves to the public with much more attractive behavior and outfit than when they are with their spouse and family. Some, in spite of their marital commitments, may allow themselves the freedom to have, against their religious instructions, passionate feelings towards others.

If large numbers of people get accustomed to these misconducts, an important section of the society may gradually forget what true chastity and the related human values are. They may become more and more corrupted, living like some animals. In turn, they can cause further deterioration of loyalty, religious behavior, family structure, trust, decent education, and other proper moral standards which are necessary as foundations for any society's long-lasting happiness. We ought to try aggressively to disrupt this detrimental chain of events so that our society can hopefully be cleansed from such sexual misconducts, although much effort and the time of a few generations may be required for our society to reach that goal.

The **criminals** at different levels of society with their many kinds of crimes can seriously threaten the future well-being of our world, causing irreplaceable losses and irreparable damages, taking away from the whole mass of innocent people the sense of security, the peace of mind, the comfort in their personal life, the confidence or trust towards one another and the freedom for their activities that they deserve to have. If we do not deal with the crimes with strong enough reaction, failing to punish the criminals seriously in an open manner for the education of others, we are being unreasonable and unfair.

The rate or frequency of the crimes of different kinds in any nation is an indicator of the lack of adequate punishment of the criminals by the people. If the physical punishment is practiced without undue delay and evident to the public, it should be the correct approach towards preventing or curing this very serious problem. To be able to approach the ideal point of elimination of serious crimes from the society the punishments may need to be increased to the point that the very severe early physical punishment is properly evident to the potential criminals of the society. Our failure in reducing crimes adequately is proof of our failure in meting out punishment of a radical nature.

At the same time there are many other factors in our social life that influence the frequency of crimes. Among these factors we may notice the use of alcoholic beverages and addictive drugs, the lack of proper education, the inadequacy of religious belief, the poverty, the availability of pornography, the insufficient care of the mentally ill, the abuse of the legal or judiciary system and the irresponsible behavior of some lawyers and professionals, while the most important being the lack of proper family life or, in other words, the absence of past experience of having felt the society's kindness in childhood.

In spite of these, the severe physical punishment should still be practiced in a very timely manner, and none of the above-mentioned potential factors should be used as an excuse by or for the criminal. The society and the system of justice should show an aggressive attitude with regard to trial and punishment, rather than sympathy followed by efforts to excuse the criminals. Individual members involved in the process of enforcement of law and order should not be concerned about their personal future popularity or prestige by being kind when presenting their views but should be concerned about the future of a whole generation of innocent people. Presentation of the spirit of forgiving and kindness can be practiced by the victim and the victim's agents, if they so desire. The judiciary system, to the contrary, must show a persistent, aggressive attitude, authorizing speedy and severe punishments as a mark of concern about the society's safety rather than promoting a self-image of misplaced gentleness.

It is also very important that the system try very hard to reduce the possibility of favoritism, so that an early and severe physical punishment is practiced for the criminals of any level of our society. In fact, to reduce the chance of abuse of the public positions of trust we may need to punish the officials who take advantage of those positions more strongly than the average people. For example, the physician who takes advantage of the patient who refers in confidence; the member of police who makes use of the uniform empowered with trust in doing wrongful or intentional false accusation or arrest; the judge, the religious guide, the attorney; the political figure who abuses the position for personal interests or favors; individuals working at different levels of government, the elected official who does wrong, taking advantage of entrusted authority; the highway engineer who is involved in bribery; the teacher; the contractor and the inspector, who do wrong for personal gains or to satisfy their selfish goals or the desires of others favored by them, all should receive, I believe, more serious punishment.

If we do not try to eradicate crime effectively, we may become a society so involved with it that its vicious circles very easily surround and destroy our nations. The criminals, along with the ones protecting them, may gain more and more power to the point that they gradually become the dominant force of some aspects of our society's function, placing more and more unfair pressure on our innocent people while, of course, causing an increasing amount of trouble for one another as well. To succeed properly in the fight against crime much reasoning may be required for persuasion of those responsible to change the existing laws and rules until the society approaches this problem intelligently rather than emotionally. Instead of being concerned about the rights of the criminal, we should realize that, after a trial without waste of time and as soon as there is reasonable certainty about the commitment of the crime, the rights are not for, but against the criminal, and the punishment or judgment, to be effective, should be carried out as soon as possible. We have to show in no uncertain terms that the rights of an innocent society far outweigh the rights of an individual, especially one who is a criminal who has flouted the laws and rights of the society.

Those who are sympathetic towards the criminal should be encouraged to try to visualize the scene of the crime. Those who are against capital punishment can try to envision the possibility of being present in a place when a murderer is preparing to kill some innocent individuals. If they have the means of killing that criminal, knowing that this is the only way to stop the slaughter, would they proceed to kill that person or not? In that kind of scenario a person, unless very selfish or unreasonably coward, would try to kill the murderer when it is concluded that through this act one or more innocents are being saved. The difference between being present in person at the scene of the crime and sitting in a chamber at the court of justice, for making a timely decision, is very much related to our emotional reactions or feelings. If one witnesses the accident of somebody being run over and killed by a car, the tragic scene may be remembered with ill-effect for a very long time. But if we hear brief news of an earthquake or some other disaster having killed many young and old in a distant location, this may not generate a fraction of the sadness caused by the viewed accident.

If we are responsible in taking some related action, we cannot let our emotions be in control instead of sound reasonable calculations. If we let murderers live and kill many more, and if through inadequate punishment of the other criminals we produce larger number of murderers, placing a mass of innocent people in harm's way, we may conclude that our opposition to capital punishment and our deficiencies in aggressive judgment towards criminals have all resulted from our being selfish, or perhaps that we refuse to see properly the real face of crime.

The use of **alcoholic beverages** and other **addictive substances** is injurious to the society. The society should strongly oppose the ones who are in the business of producing, distributing and offering of alcoholic beverages, tobacco, and addictive drugs other than for medical use. We may face, at times, much struggle, in advancing towards our goal if we are surrounded by many who are so used to these harmful habits that they consider their involvement a normal standard, inconsiderate of the great waste and the serious injuries our society can suffer from continuously as a result. It is illogical for the wrongdoers to have the permission of presenting any kind of advertisement about their harmful product to the public. I am amazed to see that some of these advertisements involve publications and events related to sports. We have to insist on offering encouragement to those who refrain from the use of these products and keep discouraging young and old from ever becoming involved with them, since the best way to quit the use of any one of these substances is to avoid the very first experience of being introduced to it.

Gambling has been, for a very long time, a source of misery for many. It has caused tremendous waste of time and manpower for those who have been engaged in it and those who have spent their efforts in its preparation or presentation. It has caused individuals and families to lose their security, their belongings, their happiness, and at times their sanity or even their lives. Those who get attracted to gambling may be fooled in having a sense of temporary pleasure, and if expecting to win, they know there is always a greater chance of losing. If they use it as entertainment, they know it comes with much risk of stress and later sadness.

It is obviously wrong to get involved with gambling when it is clear that if any advantage can be assigned to it, this would be negligible compared to its potential harmfulness. It generates false hope for the individuals and causes the majority to lose, while making many people sorry, though it could be too late for trying to compensate their losses. If there are any imaginary benefits for the society through gambling, they cannot have any final value as gambling does not serve any real useful purpose for all, except wasting society's valuable time and causing serious and at times irreparable injuries. How nice it would be if we would encourage one another to avoid becoming engaged in the use of games of chance with involvement of any small or large sums of money or other valuables. How nice if the society, in general, and we as the members of this society, would behave towards the gamblers, and especially those who are promoting this act, in such a way that they would be seriously discouraged from continuing to hurt the future of our society with this evil play that makes many individuals poor, but lets a few rich ones become wealthier.

Another problem that may have deleterious effect on our society as a vicious circle is the wide or widening **financial and power gap**. Again I want to insist on not generalizing my comments about such groups, as we have many wealthy and influential individuals and organizations offering their priceless services to the society. At the same time there are, I believe, in different nations of our world many who are using their financial or other power, regardless of the type of regime or local customs and governments, to better guarantee the continuation or exaltation of their influence. They have the capacity for manipulating the rules of nations, and they manipulate the rules in the direction of increasing their own capabilities. In this way instead of the mass of people being content with their life, securing longer lasting health of the society, there may be an increasing number of problems of different kinds for the majority of people due to such widening of the power and financial gap.

Large sums of money are being assigned to a few to further guarantee their dominance, yet without reassuring their true happiness. While they are using, for their daily life, only a small fraction of the enormous wealth which is in their control, they struggle very hard to keep it out of the reach of others in their nation who have to live with much hardship to be able to pay back the amount that they may manage to borrow for their essential expenses, together with the extra charge that is needed to augment that wealth. The rich become richer, causing larger number of decent productive families to lose more of their assets and income or to be forced into real financial breakdown. Those who are already influential gain more power so that a smaller minority controls larger majorities, generating increasing dissatisfaction among the nations, with more crime and other social problems, to the point of possible collapse of the society.

It is indeed a sad phenomenon to observe the big organizations' becoming bigger at the expense of many viable and successful small businesses of the past becoming obsolete. The wonderful people in the communities gradually lose the human contact, becoming part of a large functioning machine to the advantage of the owners of the extra large businesses or the extra large owners of those businesses. Again I want to insist on not stereotyping, as many successful owners and managers of large businesses offer tremendous help with good intentions for their employees and the whole society.

At the same time there seem to be the ones who are particularly concerned about the magnitude of the worldly wealth belonging to them and to their close ones. For the sake of increasing an already very large income, they may promote changes in the structure of the business, making many of their people lose their jobs which may be the only work they know well. Those who know best how to make money, inconsiderate of comparable service performed, may run businesses that generate large income for them alone but are harmful to the nations, endangering the future of the society. Or they may take control of other businesses and professions unrelated to their knowledge or expertise, extracting their own profit to the expense of much loss or misery for those professionals and their clientele. As mentioned elsewhere in this book, we as individuals and as nations should orchestrate ways of discouraging our people, in appropriate ways, from causing or promoting the widening gaps mentioned above.

The **lack of a healthy value system and proper family life** may be mentioned as another factor that can become a vicious circle, causing the destruction of any nation. The children who grow up in a family, feeling from the very early days of life their mother's love, then during their growth absorbing continuously from parents, or if living with other concerned individuals from those benevolent elders, with their splendid capacity for learning, the appropriate behavior and manners with responsibilities expected from them, as respected members of decent families or groups, will probably have much better chance of becoming, when grown up, successful in living with honor, having a sense of duty towards their society. But children who are growing up on the streets without any family structure or other responsible elders to offer the needed affection together with education and discipline, unless they possess strong and inherently admirable personal qualities with self-motivation for learning good deeds and emulating better role models, will become adults with a number of behavioral complexes, in turn becoming bad examples while worsening the atmosphere of education for the next generation.

The deficiency in family values when a child does not belong to a family unit with parents or other elders who can fulfill the responsibilities adequately, or when there is serious misconduct on the part of individual members of the family unit towards one another and in dealing with the society, can cause the building blocks to be placed so incorrectly in the innocent young mind that the whole construction of the future standards of life of that individual will become crooked and very difficult for structural repair later in life. With proper improvement of the structure of family life in our nations together with its related affections, moral values, and the needed discipline, many of the serious problems of our society can be successfully corrected or prevented.

While the degree of unselfishness of many individuals and groups in our time can be quite impressive, at the same time many others at different levels of our society present an attitude of **selfishness**, a quality, which is a serious problem with the capacity of reinforcing itself, and if not fought aggressively, it becomes stronger as time goes by. How nice it is if in our daily lives whenever somebody treats us in an unfair and selfish manner, we learn the beneficial lesson of not behaving the same way towards others. Instead, in many instances there seems to be the reverse effect with some of us becoming more selfish in response. This is expected since we human beings are different in character, all of us not reacting the same way in response to similar actions. The same is true in other circumstances, for example, the young one who has an alcoholic parent may become impressed with observing the related miseries and never drink alcohol, or may keep the parent's company and live likewise. The child who has been abused may become a very kind parent, when grown up, or may become a child abuser.

We can see a variety of manifestations of our selfishness when observing the life of our generation. To be nice to others is easy and does not cost anything, yet so many of us have a bitter attitude towards the others unless we have some selfish reasons for treating them nicely. As we are living in a society, we should appreciate the general feeling of the need for dealing with one another almost continuously. In this social interrelationship, there are some among us who treat others with an unfriendly attitude, being generally not nice. This by itself can cause a chain of reactions with reduction of the absolute value of the society's happiness. People can also show arrogance, especially when being needed by others, although when in need they may be flattering. Some of us, during our daily dealings with the society, are very concerned about our own privileges or advantages, ignoring the same for others to the point that gives us the feeling as if the members of our society are behaving against one another, being concerned only about the security of ourselves and those close to us.

Of course, with this attitude each individual may strive for self-centered benefits against other close ones. Our selfish behavior can sometimes be observed in very simple things that we do, such as cutting unfairly in the line of people who have been waiting or are patiently following one another, or when we watch how some people drive on the roads taking advantage of others, causing inconvenience for many.

We see the attitude of selfishness at times related to financial gains. Our religious instructions encourage us to self-sacrifice in the way of helping, financially and otherwise, those in need. While a lot of people are willing to suffer hardship for the sake of the pleasure of others, it seems that many of our individuals are so concerned about the material assets of this world that they are prepared to cause unfair damage, emotional, financial or otherwise, of larger magnitude to others in an attempt to gain some smaller value of benefit for themselves. The ultimate result of what is done by this latter group is clearly a loss to the society.

Some, with the encouragement received from some of the legal advisors, keep trying unjustly to find ways of having claims against others, with the misconception that the more they can get the better financial stability may come for their future. This may gradually cause escalation of distrust with diminution of mutual confidence and friendship. If we let this behavior persist among us, not only would we be wasting much valuable time and effort in hurting one another without any final gains for all, but we may even gradually reduce the collective value of joy and comfort of the people and with it cause the decline of our productivity, ultimately causing serious damage to the future of our society.

In the family unit, the selfish attitude of some members can have serious consequences. A parent may ruin the child's whole future for momentary pleasures, whether due to temporary selfishness without knowing how to deal with the spouse, or wrong social acquaintance, or the use of addictive substances, or losing temper to the point of causing serious emotional or physical injury to another member, or simply by being so busy with fulfilling selfish needs that the responsibilities towards the family are forgotten or ignored. As a result of such selfish behavior of any parent or child, the whole family may suffer difficulties. If this is of a serious magnitude, the complications of the life of that family unit can become long-lasting, perhaps causing, directly and indirectly, problems for others in the society as well.

We may show our selfish characteristic in being nice to the ones who admire us, even if falsely, and treating unjustly the ones who criticize us, even if appropriately. Some of us are very occupied in backbiting, criticizing, exaggerating or falsifying what others do without seeing our own mistakes. Some are accustomed to glorifying others in their presence, but magnify their faults in their absence. We may present our selfishness in that when we have done something wrong to anyone, we try to make excuses or blame others, instead of admitting our mistakes or wrongs and trying to correct ourselves. In our community when somebody is treated unfairly by our colleagues at work or other dear ones at home or outside, we protect and defend our own people, ignorant of true justice.

At the present time, with the selfishness and greed of many of our people, more or less in almost every country or part of the world, we are making life so difficult for ourselves and for one another that our society can continuously suffer from a lot of unnecessary stress to the point that many people do not enjoy the daily life but are just struggling to keep going on. Some people have so many emotional problems, almost continuously, that they lack proper mental or physical health. We are, as a society, torturing unnecessarily many of our individuals and groups through acts of selfishness and greed of our own individuals and groups. In turn, the ones who are causing mental torture and suffering to many are themselves in stress and mental anguish by the selfish acts of others.

We are doing all of this to ourselves and to each other, as we are concerned about the material life of this world, or without thinking properly we are lost in it, to the point that we do not follow the right path in order to gain from this very life even a portion of true, long-lasting and satisfying pleasure. We are striving to satisfy our pleasure of the moment without self-sacrifice in helping others to make life more enjoyable for all of us and also without sense of forgiveness or tolerance towards what actions of others we don't like when they appear to be against our own apparent interests. These observations may be true in the life of the people of any level in our society. Many successful individuals of our generation with higher status or abundance of worldly assets are feeling the same stress. Some, who are a source of misery for others, are suffering continuously from a magnitude of problems they have generated for themselves or the troubles caused to them by others, perhaps even by the ones belonging to their own class. So much stress and suffering for our people could be avoided, while we could perhaps all enjoy our time very much if each of us would try not to be selfish or greedy but to adapt to the wonderful human qualities which are clearly beneficial to the future comfort and stability of the society.

19

Last but not Least

Of the many other possible vicious circles of our society the last one that I would like to include in this section of the book is a portion of what the broadcasting and publication industries present to our people. Through the powerful informative effect of the books, journals, newspapers, magazines, recordings of different kinds, movies, computer assisted telecommunications, radio, television and related products, our young and old are continuously learning a tremendous magnitude of useful new information. Much of this knowledge is needed for our society's proper function, together with words of wisdom that help in guiding us on how to live right and to put our physical and mental capabilities to correct use. At the same time, through the same means of communication, I believe a very large volume of material that can be seriously harmful if presented to the public is being produced and in an unfair manner made available to the people. This latter portion of their service, which I call disservice, is strongly threatening the future well-being of our society.

Since in this book I am looking with a critical view to discuss what changes should be recommended for improvement of our society, I do not intend to detail the good parts of media presentations but to write about the harmful ones which they present to our society and the wrong that they do to our future. I have a strong feeling that from the above–mentioned industries, in the present life-span of our society, perhaps television, with presentation of some very harmful programs, is the one with the most corruptive influence on the different age groups of our people and on different nations in the world. Yet, there is an invisible line of cooperation somehow connecting many of these broadcasting and publishing means to one another, in their success with encouragement or support of each other for supplying this kind of harmful product, and for their poisoning the minds of our society to the point of having these products easily accepted. The complex or complicated vicious circle formed by them includes, involves, and reinforces all of the vicious circles mentioned in the preceding paragraphs, and perhaps many more. They keep bombarding us repeatedly with what is seriously damaging to the future well-being of our society, to the point that a significant population of our society becomes accustomed to that wrong and expects to have more of it presented, which then worsens the productions of the media to the degree that it results in moral or other deteriorations we see in our society.

Though a few, and not all, of the people in broadcasting and publishing industries with their influence, cause many aspects of the corruption of our society, in due course those few people receive from their partially corrupted customers, encouragement for continuation of same or stronger dose of their poisons. Their production then increases to supply larger numbers of harmful products, as they are, in a selfish way, concerned about the quantity of customers they can please, rather than caring about the quality of their service to a nobler audience among their customers. If they present repeatedly the wrongdoings without strong enough criticism, or with failure to show their untoward outcomes, not only would they be letting many of us learn the bad lesson of how to do wrong but they are also helping the society adapt gradually to the indecent acts, becoming more and more accustomed to what we should try to refrain from for the sake of being good and doing better. If they bring to us what we emotionally enjoy seeing and hearing, though it is logically deleterious to the future betterment of the whole society, still their main concern being the attraction of larger number of customers, unfortunately through what they do they promote increase in the degree of stress and misery for the present and future society of mankind.

In this way, the dangerous chain of reactions becomes stronger, and a vicious circle brings future miseries to our nations. The members of the society are so involved with and adapted to the vices that they do not feel how their mind is being gradually poisoned, nor can they see how the circle of the vices is with a powerful serpentine action, tightening its grip more and more to the point of crushing them along with their society.

I would like to discuss this subject further while mentioning briefly some of these wrongs which are presented to a society, or a few of the ones that are capable of forming vicious circles, endangering a society's future stability and happiness, even though part of this would be a repetition of what is mentioned elsewhere in this book.

A very serious and basic problem with the broadcasting and publishing industries is the abuse by some of their people of the expression of freedom of speech, which should be practiced, only, and I repeat only, for the expression of opinions. While they must have and we all want to have, freedom to express our opinions, they should never be freely permitted to publish or present every material that they choose without observation of appropriate ethical standards of conduct. There should be freedom for the expression of an opinion but not for using whatever obscene language or sexually compromising pictures and scenes in the presentation of an opinion. They should not be allowed to present to the public words or pictures which are wanting in modesty or void of our moral and ethical values, or what according to sensible and logical reasoning would have an adverse effect on the society's future.

It does not make sense that certain programs in television, because of showing violence or erotic scenes or unethical words and suggestions, are considered not suitable for being watched by children. I have the same objection in regard to the other published or broadcast erotic materials which are categorized, because of the same reason, for adults only. Not only are many children and adolescents seeing in television, cinema, publications and elsewhere immoral scenes or pictures which are supposedly prepared for the grown-ups, they are reading inappropriate printed materials which are all sources of mental and physical harm to them and great damage to the future of their society, but these products can be the cause of serious problems for the adults, too.

The availability of such materials, whether immoral writings or some pictures and scenes, which are in whatever manner stimulating or misguiding the readers or viewers away from the right path, can be harmful for any age group. The argument that as grown-ups we are free to view and read whatever pictures and writings we want to, and the ones in control of their production are free to produce any materials they desire, putting them within our reach with our having the choice of what to view and what not to, all these are self-defeating debates.

The very important basic attitude for individuals' and the society's well-being is that we are to refrain from doing what is wrong, according to a variety of principles, in spite of our momentary desire for doing it. We also need to be persistent in practicing this very important human quality of self-control, so that it becomes for us an easy routine, and perhaps gradually more of a deep satisfaction and joy when we keep from doing what is wrong and instead try to be good and doing what is right according to those principles. The more we let ourselves be free to have access to the temptations which can pull us back towards the harmful inclinations, regardless of our age, the more possibility for our regression towards moral default, followed by the untoward consequences for us and our society.

It is a lie if we claim that the availability of those harmful products, whether written or broadcast materials of our society, and our reading, hearing and watching them freely without self-restraint, have no bad effect or misguiding influence on us. It is equally wrong if the ones who prepare and offer those harmful productions say that it is not their fault if they present those materials to the public since the people have the choice of making use of them or not.

For example, some say that when we see a program on television which is, according to our judgment, harmful to be watched, we have the switch to keep the television on or off. This is a completely invalid excuse, since many of us, at whatever age, when faced with the availability of harmful but attractive products, may succumb to the temptations. With repetition we can gradually become used to them, followed by impairment of our preexisting principles and possible deterioration of our character to a point which would have been totally unacceptable to our previous sound judgment. Except for the presentation of the opinions, their freedom in making their productions available to the public should be under strict control of the rules or guidelines set forth by the committees of the appointed and qualified individuals who are concerned about the future life of mankind on this planet, while neither the ones who set the rules nor those who enforce them would have personal financial or similar interests in the sale of the productions.

The publishing and broadcasting industries need to be receiving this kind of continuous guidance or advice since they are so trusted by their customers that their mistakes can manipulate the minds and lives of the nations inappropriately, causing at times very serious consequences. Their freedom to present to the society whatever they desire is totally illogical since we know that their inappropriate product can have adverse effects on the lives of many. In our civilization we try to prevent anyone's intentional harm to another innocent human being. We also try very hard to protect large masses of people against any harm. When there is danger to innocent people, we see that, if needed, a few are sacrificed for the sake of many, such as in war, making brave soldiers march into danger to safeguard their nations, or in the process of punishment of criminals, when occasional innocents may be inadvertently included among the criminals by way of securing the safety of the whole community. I may conclude that it is wrong to sacrifice and endanger the future well-being of our nations and the whole society for the profit of small groups.

Those who knowingly participate in the preparation, distribution and offering of any material which is ultimately harmful to the future of the society should feel guilty about placing a trap to catch some innocent people. They are furnishing the bait, which is attractive, while they are interested in making profit from their catch, but careless about the serious injuries that the trap can inflict on the ones who are caught. How could they claim to be not guilty of setting the trap? At the same time, the ones who go after the bait knowing of their wrongdoing or realizing the possible resultant complications, must share the blame. For many others, perhaps of the younger age group, who are trapped, when attracted by the bait, unaware of the undesirable consequences, by the time they notice their injuries it may be too late for trying to return to the healthy free world.

The responsible parties of that portion of the publishing and broadcasting industries who are causing, through their production of harmful materials in the world, a variety of consequences injurious to our society and its future should feel guilt in their conscience for what they do. Through what they present, they seem to be trying to weaken our ethical, moral, cultural, and religious standards. They bring to us the wrong and sinful part of the life of the society, as if they are trying to get us used to that kind of behavior. They present to us the criminal and the sexual deviant in such a way as if they are forcing us to accept them instead of trying to have our society cleansed of them. They offer the material that stimulates the young ones to become, at an early age, physically attracted to one another with strong sexual passions, or the elders to forget the shame of having unethical physical and sexual acts. They persist in making available to us erotic or romantic vocabulary and scenes that can be a source of much stimulation and arousal of out-of-place temptations, which can also have serious negative influence on the properly needed physical attraction that should exist between the ones who are rightly committed to each other with their romantic ties and marriage vows.

They present what can be totally inappropriate for public use, inconsiderate of their causing much gradual deterioration of behavior of any age groups, much indecency among the young ones or the old, many unwed pregnancies, much sexually transmitted disease and related emotional problems, and a large magnitude of criminal acts related to all of these social complications. They keep insisting that they are free to present all of it, and they claim that according to their statistics and studies they are not responsible for these results. They place the trap and the bait without showing any guilt or without admitting to their being responsible for injuring their catch, which is ultimately the whole society.

I consider much of what we do illogical. There is a strong relationship between their sexual presentations and the resultant indecencies practiced by part of the society, such as the rapes, kidnappings, and other related crimes and sexual misbe-haviors. We permit them the freedom to do this harm to us, then we complain of suffering from the results. Then we try to catch those who have been committing the related sexual crimes. If we succeed in arresting them, we spend much of the society's time and effort in finding some excuse for clearing them of the blame, releasing them, sooner or later, unharmed into the society. Often their misguiding presentations are available even to the guilty one who is in incarceration.

To attract larger numbers of the members of the younger generation they try to please their customers by offering in their products an attitude of rebellion. They encourage the young, at an age when they are vulnerable and have high self-confidence for knowledge, but weak when faced with temptations, to adopt a rebellious character against traditional standards of society. They promote rebellion in the way the youngsters may dress, listen to music and choose their enter-tainment, or they gradually cause their encouragement to rebel against the older cultural, moral, and ethical principles of parents, teachers, and a conservative, cautious society, or to rebel against the governments and the established social dis-cipline and many other aspects of the lives of the more senior or older members of society.

This attitude of rebellion is against one of the essential principles of our civilization which is the application of the result of the older experiences, or what the generations have gradually learned, to our lives. Instead of encouraging the young to be improperly different, they should cooperate in harmony with their benevolent colleagues in discouraging this rebellious attitude, because, while we as members of the society need to pursue inventions, discoveries or learning new things, it does not mean we should ignore or disregard the good old things, so that we do not waste our time in this life in repeating the mistakes of others, being careless about what has been already learned and established through expe-rience.

They ought to help in preparing an atmosphere of coop-eration between the older and younger generations, so that those who are on their way to form the society of the future, pay attention to the positive and negative outcomes of what has been done by others before them, then carefully apply the results to their lives, continuing to perform right but avoiding repeating the mistakes of others. Such examples as listening to the elders who are sorry for smoking cigarettes or having other harmful addictions which they cannot quit easily, wishing that they would never have started, or the child accepting the advice when the parent, who finds no easy way for removing the tattoo of an inappropriate picture or writing from distant past, recommends caution before deciding to do what may have an important and long- lasting effect. To please many customers, at least temporarily, some promote the attitude of feeling free from a variety of established standards or obligations, finding this trick appealing among the younger generation. Freedom, democracy, independence, and similar words are nice titles used by them when they are playing with our emotions. Actually as we are human beings our freedom should be under the control of some nobler human qualities and standards. We do not live like animals with the feeling that we are free to do as we wish whenever we feel like it.

They convert almost every aspect of our life to entertainment, again for pleasing or attracting larger groups of customers. To achieve this purpose they present events of news that should not be brought to the public but to the proper authorities only, or they may exaggerate to make something more interesting, or they produce fascinating misguiding news out of a rumor, or they present the news in such a way that a variety of problems can be triggered for the society, while they are trying to entertain larger numbers of people with their news. They portray the evil face of violence or crime under the garb of entertainment to the point of making many accustomed to it. They change something wonderful such as sport into entertainment, to the point of encouraging a few to play it in a dangerous and violent manner so as to make it more attractive to some, while having many waste their time in watching it rather than participating in healthy physical exercise. They entertain with the showing of some seriously wrong aspects of family life, to the point of ruining the friendship and trust which are expected to keep the bond among family members, the fidelity that should exist between spouses, and the mutual respect and close ties which are needed between children and their responsible elders.

Instead, they ought to present beautiful and trustworthy aspects of the life of the family unit, so as to encourage our young ones to proceed towards the formation of family life with greater optimism and enthusiasm. The normal family, which is established through sincere and intimate association of two persons of opposite sex, who try to satisfy cooperatively, with their existing physiological differences, their combined social and other needs, in order to become better members of society, and bring into existence possible future offspring possessing optimal qualities of body and mind, leading to a healthy and happy continuation of the existence of mankind in this world.

They produce entertainment out of being unfairly disrespectful towards others and to those in responsible positions, resulting in diminution of the prestige necessary for the work of those officials; towards many other professionals, resulting in loss of the necessary confidence that the clients in general should feel in dealing with those professionals; towards different ethnic groups, resulting in disturbance of the friendly relationship among the members of our society; and towards other decent individuals with admirable qualities who deserve respect rather than entertaining but rude remarks.

They ought to examine critically their wrong entertainment policies and follow the footsteps of others who are presenting entertainment which is adequate both in quality and quantity, free from vices and often educational, as this can help our society's well-being and productivity. They should keep from offering entertainment which is attracting attention but wasting much of people's valuable time and being totally useless or perhaps containing what can be a source of moral or other deterioration. This kind of entertainment hurts the society and its productivity, not only causing much waste of time of the young and old who are being entertained, but also through its bad effect on the minds and actions of those people later on. They present words and writings or pictures and scenes which are seriously unsuitable for any age group of our people to become accustomed to. Even in what has been specially prepared for the very young we may find violence, romance or other stimulating presentations that can cause very serious complexes later and the inappropriate written or spoken language that we may criticize our growing generation for speaking.

They present some individuals' or groups' useless achievements as true service to the society, or perhaps persons who have done wrong or possess qualities against our decent human values, showing them as if they are happy with what they have done; or they present with enthusiasm devious individuals, letting them become, with their faulty characteristics, role models to our innocent young. To make their presentations draw the attention of as many eyes and ears as possible they let the individuals present words that should not be used in public and pictures and scenes with immoral contents or indecently exposed bodies. At times they show their benevolence with presenting a documentary to criticize some wrong production of others, only to abuse the occasion attracting the attention of many, while making available, under the mask of criticism, the very devious material which should not have been presented in the first place.

These individuals may falsely imitate their honest colleagues in presenting themselves as truly an unbiased voice of the people, then using their selfish attitude or their bias they may convince masses of their nations, in whatever part of our world, for or against whom they desire, or in positive or negative advocation of whatever they like or dislike. Their work or word has strong impact on the minds of their people when they claim that what they present are the people's feelings or expectations. In this way they successfully stimulate or arouse groups and nations in favor or against individuals or other groups. How wonderful it could be if they would make strong effort to overcome their prejudice and selfishness, then they would join their wonderful colleagues in using the very effective tool which is at their disposal, for reaching the large masses of people in different parts of our world in an appropriate way, aiming, in an unselfish manner, to serve the society and trying to improve the quality of the future life of mankind.

Our society is in serious trouble with a variety of problems threatening its future well-being. We need to cooperate in an unselfish way to strive towards saving our society from its grave sickness. We can compare our status to the crowd of people in a secluded place with spreading fire nearby, when there is a door through which they can all exit to safety with orderly progress, cooperation, and unselfishness. Yet, through selfishness and by trying to force their way out without concern about the safety of others, they may be burned as a group, together with those who feel they may be successful in saving themselves by pushing others back into the fire. If we do not try to cleanse our society of crime, promiscuity, homosexuality, pornography, the abuse of alcohol and drugs, gambling, and many other vices with which we are involved in different degrees in all countries of our world, the future of the life of mankind on earth is faced with disasters.

I do not mean to exhibit any feeling of dislike towards the persons who are involved in serious wrongdoing, but to bring to their notice how terrible their actions can be and how serious the consequences. I also want them to understand the logical viewpoint that there should be aggressive and severe reaction against their wrong actions for the sake of saving the society's future. This does not reflect any judgment on the quality of their real personality. We are human beings; no one is perfect. I have done good and bad, and if I live long enough, probably I will be doing much good and many bad actions in the future. Yet I am trying to do better and to stay away from the vices.

My plea is not against the criminals but against their wrongdoing. I can even make the request to any criminal who may see this writing that you please realize the seriousness of what you have done and please accept from the society and the system of justice the severe enough punishment, evident to the public, adequate to be used as a deterrent, a lesson for the other potential criminals. Please, remember that for the sake of the safety of so many living on this planet you can accept the consequence of your own serious wrongdoing. To the homosexuals I can request that you please understand, I am not against you but against the sinful action which we should try to eradicate. Paying attention to religious beliefs, this can be considered a shame for those accustomed to it and filth for the involved society. Please, notice the magnitude of your diversion from the right path. I request that you stop your sinful acts and repent to God Almighty by seeking forgiveness.

If we let the elements of deterioration of our society with their vicious cycles remain functional, they may continue to gain force. While our nations are suffering injuries from the effect of the storm of wrongdoings, these destructive powers, reinforcing one another in an atmosphere which is void of proper faith, admirable human values and decent behaviors may gradually form a powerful twist that can destroy our nations and the wonderful society of mankind on this planet.

For correction of our society's serious problems we need to have the cooperation and strong dedication of our people. No matter where on this planet, with their own political system enforced and whatever kind of government being in power, those who have the official authorities and the assigned responsibilities, even with the help of religious and community leaders, may not succeed in the abolition of our moral or social problems without people's help. The correction needs to be started in our society, God willing, as soon as possible, by the individuals of each nation.

When a large mass of our people tries, with adequate courage and good intention, to help each other in improving the values and performance of our society, we may see that the individuals with higher authority in each country not only will cooperate with the society but will be very pleased to do so. They are, after all, none but members of the same society, and when we all try together to correct our deficiencies, we can enjoy watching the society's functioning happily and our own work being done much more smoothly. Instead of our being fascinated with too much of the wasteful luxuries of this world for some to the expense of the suffering of many, the whole society can enjoy an attitude of cooperation, with each individual's persistent effort towards living right and assisting others in performing well, feeling proper contentment and having adequate pleasures in life.

20

cA very Simple Logic, Presented to the Unbelievers

It is everybody's obligation to try to live right, perform appropriately according to logic, and be as good as possible. This is true in the case of those who have the understanding of and faith in the existence of soul and the hereafter and are wise enough to strive towards perfection of the way they live in this world, since these people try to follow the religious instructions and the ethics of a sensible society. The others, who neither believe in The Creator Of All Beings, nor accept the fact of existence of our soul and the eternal life, still have to be good and do what is right for the whole society. Let me elaborate on this issue of why those people, who only believe in the material aspect of our life, still have to try doing good and living correctly.

If they do not accept the fact that each of us, besides having a body of matter that is engaged in the biochemical phenomena and processes of life, has also a soul or inner non-material person who has the feelings and the individual capacity of decision making, then they are accepting to be each of them, for the time being, just an object or a physical piece of this planet. In this way they deny the separate individual values of their person. Therefore, on the one hand, they should not attach any importance to their feelings of joy, sorrow, pain or pleasure, as these would be only some electrochemical changes and orderly impulses or reactions in their body, comparable to some less complicated processes of the world, such as the changes in the atmosphere during a storm, when one may assume that there is no concern, such as when portions of a cloud may suffer from feeling the heat of the lightning. On the other hand, through this disbelief they discredit the identity of every one of them being truly a separate functioning unit while considering that a continuous exchange exists between their substance and the surrounding matter that is in contact with them and remembering their biological attachment to others through the chain of the process of reproduction. So, they are accepting to be only a part of this material world and its functions.

These people still believe in the need for some order in the functions of the material world, so they must accept or respect the different levels of that order. They expect the smaller and less important portions of the matter in this life to keep functioning right and, if needed, tolerate difficulties or be sacrificed as a way to guarantee the adequate function of the larger or more important physical beings. They agree that all of the parts of their body have to function correctly in trying to help their whole physical person stay healthy. Even parts of the body may tolerate difficulties or, if needed, self-sacrifice and die in the effort towards supporting the continuation of the proper functioning of the related organs or systems and that person as a sound unit. The white blood cells may attack the infecting organism in an area and become part of the abscess and expelled pus. The cells of the skin become part of a dead supporting cover in the way to protect the body from the outside hazardous influences. These people accept the fact that parts of their body have to tolerate difficulties to support other parts. They expect their hands and feet and muscles to suffer from tiredness, pain, blisters, and at times injuries, in the process of their trying to reach what may provide more security and comfort in life for the whole body, whether this would be during the struggle to earn needed sustenance or in the process of getting access to a desired object or place, recognition or fame, or some achievement in sport.

Through life they expect that every individual part or portion of their body should struggle to function right towards the advantages of the more major parts and the whole body. Therefore, since they accept being only parts of the material world surrounding them without any soul, with their feelings being only part of the physical phenomena in the area, without any individual personal significance, they must accept the simple and very clear conclusion that they too have to strive in doing what is right and advantageous for future well-being of their communities and ultimately the whole society and the planet earth. Any individual who disregards the processes and principles mentioned above and continues to be irrationally selfish can be considered as a diseased part that can contribute to causation of sickness for the whole body.

21

Those who
Rightly Deserve

Throughout this book I have been trying to present my
feelings about how we, as individuals or as groups, are helping
or hurting our society while the effects of what we do influence
our own lives, the lives of others and of the future inhabitants
of this world. We should try to have courage, not only to
correct our own mistakes so that we may improve the future of
our society, but also to encourage others to do the same. This
needs to be a cooperative effort by all of us as the members of
the large family of mankind living on earth. We ought to refrain
from being, in a selfish manner, concerned about our own advantage and inconsiderate of the privileges of other people,
whether as an individual behaving against those around us or as
a group against other groups of the whole society on this
planet. Perhaps it is time for us to stop hurting each other in our
communities and all over the world and to start helping our
fellow mankind towards making better use of our world, resulting in an increase of availability of comfort for all people to
the point that we may have adequate collective value of happiness for our whole society.

We are all concerned about the health of this society, as we
are part of it. Also, its future must be of utmost importance to
us, as it directly affects the living condition of future generations who have at least among them the individuals whom we
like very much in one way or another even before they are
born.

After having recognized, with logical reasoning, the factors
that help the future well-being of our society, it seems very reasonable to expect that our society should try to devise means to
encourage those factors, while supporting the individuals who
are promoting them. At the same time, the society should insist

on having ways to fight the factors which are in the long run
detrimental to the health of our society and to discourage the
ones who are supporting those factors.

It is not right that we honor the individuals for their
achievements in only worldly matters, but useless in the way of
true service to the society. Perhaps, at times, some individuals
have earned respect with fame even through having done what
can be harmful or wrong. Some may gain popularity for their
physical or other inherent characteristics and capabilities.
Many are admired because of their degree of success in
reaching higher worldly standards or gaining control over
larger amounts of the assets of this world.

To have a better chance for a happy future, our society in
general should devise ways of supporting those who are doing
their fair share in properly serving the society while discouraging members who carelessly or in a selfish way are
source of damage to the society. The degree of support or
respect that we offer individuals or groups should not be according to our being impressed emotionally with how their
physical appearance is, what their capabilities are, or what they
have in their possession, irrespective of how good is their
service to the society or how well they mean to perform it. Nor
should they be honored without taking into consideration the
quality of their personal, moral, and ethical values.

If somebody has become wealthy by intentionally doing
what is wrong to the society, that person should clearly feel the
disrespect and rejection of the society rather than enjoy any
honor for wealth. We should not honor an individual for mere
wealth, but for how that wealth has been earned and how it is
being spent in serving and helping others. We should not honor
a person merely for having more influence in worldly matters,
but for how that influence is being used in making life easier
and happier for others and for the whole society.

It does not make logical sense that we, as individuals or as
groups, respect some other individuals or groups because of
their being **famous or rich**. We show them our support or we
honor them with a lot of enthusiasm, even on some occasions
that we see their performance has been aiming to hurt the
society for their personal gains. Some may have become
famous or rich by having done what can damage the educa-

tional, ethical, financial, medical, moral, or other standards of our society. In fact, there should be a negative value of respect for wealth or fame alone without the needed accompanying admirable human qualities. It seems to be wrong when we honor somebody or some group for having had much success while we can understand that the result of what they have done is detrimental to the future well-being of our society. It is like my admiring somebody's nice outfit while I know that person has stolen it from me.

I do not mean to say that being famous or rich is wrong, but I would like to insist that there should not be any admiration just for fame or wealth, but rather for the way people become famous and for how they earn their wealth and what they do with it. We ought to submit aggressively to this kind of attitude in order to save the future of our society. To support some wrongdoers simply because we are fascinated with their luxurious presentation is wrong. For nourishing the insects with its flowers, if a plant attracts such insects that help spread the pollen and assist in the reproduction of that plant, this process improves the chances for the future existence of that kind of plant. If, on the other hand, a plant does not fight against but supports with nourishment some beautiful large or small animals and worms that can rapidly eat the leaves, causing destruction of that plant, the outcome may be serious, causing scarcity or even extinction of the said plant. We must clearly show that the success in getting the support of the society depends on how good we are, not on how much goods we control.

In our present civilization apparently a very small portion of the people in the world is in control of a very large percentage of its finances. If we agree that among the majority, who are struggling to make a living, there are vast numbers of people who are engaged in doing work which is much more productive or useful for the society than what some individuals from the minority of the very wealthy or famous are doing, we can then agree that showing disrespect and rejection for such wealth which is earned without intention of serving a society and for the fame gained through achievements in contradiction to the long-lasting health of a society will help to encourage a better future for the coming generations.

It does not make sense that a farmer and family when working hard together and supplying our much needed food, do not make enough money to have a life half as comfortable as some individuals involved in production, distribution, and sale of substances which are clearly detrimental to the sanity and safety of our society. I cannot see much fairness in our not supporting some well–qualified and dedicated educators, who are helping to build the strong foundations of our future world while many of us support with much wealth and luxury the groups and the locations that promote gambling and promiscuity.

Parents in our society can show their children how together, with mutual cooperation, they can donate their time and assistance to the **schools** and other facilities dedicated to education. At the same time the children may enjoy proper hobbies and entertainments while being discouraged from supporting the people and places that gather these fresh and innocent minds and bodies, leading them to waste their time in listening to loud and harmfully stimulating sounds of undisciplined music, jumping up and down to its rhythm, having indecent outfit and behavior, and while there exists the tendency of their encouraging one another to use some addictive substances and getting involved in immoral actions.

The news **media** with the powerful effect of radio and television, the newspapers, magazines, books and other publications, the cinema, and related industries, all have very strong influence on our daily lives, on how we feel individually and about others, on how we perform at home and at work, on how we behave towards our family members and our friends, or towards strangers nearby and in faraway parts of the world. They also have tremendous influence on the education and behavior of our young ones who are the future society of this world. Our society should, therefore, adopt ways of encouraging the producers of the above-mentioned materials to present to us what is good for our society's well-being and right for our long-term future.

We should aggressively discourage those among the news media who bring to us what is detrimental to our society. Their reasoning, that they are free to present what they want and we are free to choose what to read or watch, is misguided. The original supporters of the freedom of speech did not mean to condone pornography or the use of foul language in public, but the freedom of being able to express one's opinion. The persons who knowingly present to us what is wrong for the society are guilty of causing our temptations by placing what is harmful within our reach. In the same way that people who prepare harmful addictive substances for improper application are at fault, so are their distributors and users. I feel sorry when I notice that possibly many of us support what is presented and their presenters, depending on the emotional or sentimental attractions rather than on wise and logical reasoning, proper self-control, and adequate concern for the future of our society.

It is also very sad if we do not have, on certain occasions, proper or strong enough means of supporting the **honest** people of our society and aggressively discouraging everybody, at whatever social level or standard of life, from dishonesty. The society ought to show with deliberate effort that the individuals and groups who try to reach their goals with dishonesty, through cheating others or deceiving an honest society, not only fail to be rewarded or honored for their undeserving achievements but, regardless of the status of their privileges in the society, they very probably face serious consequences for their misdeeds. The ones who voluntarily confess to their mistake, demonstrating with honesty and good intention their sorrow for what they have done and their will in trying not to repeat that mistake, can be forgiven. Those who are exposed of their wrongdoing against their wish should face the untoward result of their action. If some officials, politicians, or other individuals, after having had their serious unjust function disclosed involuntarily, present their regret for what they have done, the society should be firm in treating them according to their guilt without being fooled by their ability to give enchanting speeches or showing fascinating acts. This would be the right way to educate the others of comparable positions and the mass of potential wrongdoers to keep from submitting to similar mistakes and hopefully to improve the chance of our society's future integrity.

22

Parting, with Contentment

When a part of our body or an organ is removed surgically because of disease, we very quickly learn to dissociate our person from that piece, so that we do not consider it as a part of our body any more. If we look at that tissue after its removal, whether a gangrenous toe, an infected vermiform appendix, an inflamed gallbladder with its stones, a cancerous tumor or an atrophic kidney, not only do we have no more affection towards it as part of our body, but we feel glad to have that decaying piece as a dead tissue away from us, being then concerned about the well-being of the remaining body.

The degree of our concern about the removal of a part of our body varies depending on the importance of that part, the amount of difficulty in removing it, and the impairment of the function we may suffer after its removal. Losing an arm or a leg is more important than losing a short piece of the bowel, and having our tonsils removed is a bigger deal than clipping our nails. Yet, no matter how much of our tissues are removed, with whatever degree of disability resulting from it, we feel those are just some lost physical pieces, while our person or individuality remains intact.

It can be very comforting if we learn to feel about the whole of our physical body the same way, noticing that it is all made of tissues. When we have it as part of us, we look after it as well as we should. When the time comes for its separation from us, we should hopefully be prepared for leaving it. Then, there does not seem to be any room for sorrow, but concern and hope for the well-being of our real person beyond the point of that separation.

23

cAway from Prejudice, Selfishness, and Greed

Let us join in a cooperative effort towards perfecting this world. The world, as placed at our disposal, is just what we need, filled with beauties. It is we who do right and wrong or good and bad to ourselves, to each other and to this world. Let us hold hands all together in friendship as we are members of the same large family, all living in this great home under the same blue sky. Let us put our unimportant differences aside, paying attention to how much help we can offer to one another, away from prejudice, selfishness and greed. Let us feel how much we can trust each other, even when we have different ways of life or traditions when we belong to different groups for different reasons, whether we call our groups Buddhist, Christian, Hindu, Jewish, Muslim, Zoroastrian or whatever else we are named, as long as we truly believe in The One Supreme Being and the hereafter.

Through the realization of our worshipping The Same Authority we may feel closer to each other, unifying gradually into one body, rather than through worshipping separate idols, such as human figures, the religious leaders, or the prophets, causing separation of our groups from each other with an increasingly unreasonable dislike, each group insisting on its superiority or the correctness of its path while all of the others are accused of going astray.

Let us have universal plans, assisting each other to control the variety of pollutions we are dealing with, trying to keep the air, the land, and the water of this planet as clean as possible, everyone being concerned not only about the area close to where we live at the time but all of the earth. Also we must try and reduce as much as possible other existing pollutions, such as the nuisance of noise and the causes of moral deterioration.

We should have proper plans for population control all over the world. It does not make logical sense that perhaps some groups believe that through their forbidding birth control among their own people they can have a better chance of increasing their number more rapidly compared to the others. While I agree that criminal abortion must be against the religion, I have strong personal feeling that birth control, if aimed at prevention of joining of the two germ cells, each of which is incomplete for formation of a living individual, is not forbidden by God, but being a rule attached to the religion by human beings.

If we have near optimum number of people on this planet and if we become united in an unselfish manner for the sake of obeying God Almighty, following the commands given by God, as we are supposed to do, sharing with one another the more than adequate supply of goods available to us, perhaps we can see on this planet a life close to what is said to exist in paradise. Should we try to live such an almost perfect life, which could be a rehearsal of what we expect to happen in the hereafter, may, God willing, improve our chances of having a part to play in the desirable heavenly life.

24

The Leaders, and our Sacrifices

At the same time that wonderful deeds are being done by people all over the world at every moment, we are also hurting each other, both as individuals and as groups.

Many individuals are causing trouble for each other through selfishness, greed and prejudice. If we could try hard to avoid these three harmful qualities, we would probably get rid of most of the serious problems that we have in the world. We also have groups, small or large, all over this planet, who are at times, for different reasons or excuses, causing destructive damage, whether minor or major, to each other. Still the three qualities mentioned above are possibly the main energizing fuel for these harmful acts. Perhaps the most important driving force is the ambition of the ones who are controlling the groups as their leaders. These leaders encourage their group members to self-sacrifice bravely in the way of keeping their group successful, not mentioning clearly that one of their most important concerns, or possibly the most important one, is the continuation and reinforcement of their own power of leadership with its accompanying privileges.

Groups may be formed with reasons related to nationality, religion, race, profession, and a variety of other binding factors. Members of each group behave as if they want to become dominant, eliminating any competition, with the feeling that if everybody is as nice as they are, all of the other people being part of their group or under their control, then they can solve our problems which are due to lack of cooperation, leaving no more trouble among the people. Yet, when we observe individual groups, if they include large enough numbers of people, they can have their own inside mishaps. In large groups, a variety of problems may exist that can disturb their unity, due to conflict of interests of the smaller sub-groups or of the individual members. Again, each smaller group, or the individuals who are there in control, struggle to dominate, as if they can do a better job than their opponents. Since each of these groups, when large enough, has its own inside problems, it is clear that if they dominate the others there is no guarantee of having a better future for all.

As has been mentioned in this book in reference to countries and nations, if any group of people, no matter what common quality binds it together, in trying to secure its own safety, causes any unfair harm to another group, its behavior can be compared to a person who selfishly ignores the rights of another individual while committing an act of crime. Groups of people in this world simulate the behavior of the individuals of a society.

After living intimately for long enough periods of time among different groups of people of our world, we can appreciate the fact that all of our groups are, more or less, formed of the same range of mixed human qualities. No matter what makes the foundation of the group or groups that we belong to, it is unwise for us to develop a special feeling with group prejudice towards or against members of another group and treat them all alike. It is better that our groups be formed with the intention to cooperate in improving our world and the living conditions in it for its great present and future societies, rather than uniting with a bunch as a small or large team or gang, hurting another group, inconsiderate of the innocence and decency of the many we may harm. We should be tough enough to oppose the aggressors who may have the intention of taking advantage of our rights. At the same time we ought to control our emotions so that we do not attain an attitude of hate towards all of the members of a group, including the innocents, nor do we hurt the better people instead of the ones at fault. At times some individuals who are not benevolent are in the position of leadership of the groups, misguiding them with their own greed or selfish intentions, letting many nice people of various groups suffer because of the consequences of their mistakes.

Many people with admirable human qualities are prepared to serve the society but are not in a position of great influence. Instead they are manipulated, and their actions are controlled by the others. Many of the better individuals fail to present themselves and their ideas clearly in the defense of what is right, while some not so nice people, although small in number, aggressively present their wrong ideas until they can effectively convince the others, changing the opinion of the society, and of the ones in control, in their own favor.

To approach the possibility of long-lasting worldwide peace, I believe our people, while divided into large and small groups due to their religious practice, country of residence, race and many other factors, should be encouraged to cleanse their conscience of group prejudices. While we still belong to different groups, we can keep from generalizing our opinion or attitude towards all of the people of any other group. We may extend our hand of friendship towards the more benevolent people of each group. To search for wonderful individuals, we need to approach the other groups without any dislike, getting involved with them in a kind, intimate association.

If the nobler people of the world, no matter what groups they belong to, unite together, they may be able to secure a long-lasting peace all over this planet. They can form the strongest and most benevolent human power for the general good of mankind. These will be the people who are least selfish. They sacrifice their own pleasures for the betterment of the living conditions of others. These individuals serve the society for the sake of obeying God Almighty rather than for personal gains alone. Through this honorable friendship, with the powerful influence resulting from the intimate cooperation of the nicer people of our world, selfish individuals may lose their ability to manipulate the groups into wrongdoing or to position them against one another.

25

The World of Finances or Finances of the World

The subject of economy in this day and age, whether American, that of the other large countries, or the world's economy, is a very complex issue. Educated specialists and financial advisors with broad knowledge and expertise in mathematics, accounting, economics, and other related fields offer discussions which are far above my understanding about their ways of trying to make adjustments in how we handle money in our daily lives, manipulating the taxes, the interest rates and other factors that influence our economy. They make a multitude of recommendations to individuals, organizations, and governments on how to become more successful in financial planning. My brain with its little comprehension of the material cannot easily absorb those complicated discussions.

In the following paragraphs, therefore, I would like to present to the readers of this book my simple view of the subject, while referring to a variety of factors which I believe are the basic elements with direct and indirect influence on the economy or our financial contentment. With the diversity of the points of discussion, I presume the matters will be presented in some order which is not going to be perfectly organized. Yet, as this writing does not claim to be flawless nor an accurate example of the use of language, I hope readers will pay more of their kind attention to the subject of my thoughts and forgive my shortcomings in composition and use of language. Since I am trying to emphasize a variety of important issues in this section of the book, I may at times seem to get sidetracked or repetitive.

To simplify the subject for myself, I consider the financial status of the society to be clearly affected by the balance between the production and the consumption of materials and services which are essential or necessary to secure our future contentment in life and the long-lasting comfort of the coming generations. Most of our struggles in the way of playing with difficult figures and numbers for reduction of economic problems of our society would be unnecessary if we, the members of this society, cooperated with one another in producing more and wasting less.

Let me compare the economy and financial resources of the society to the food and nutrition of a large group of people who live in a big house or a compound. They have shortage of food for the whole group as their supply is only the product of their own garden or backyard and the poultry kept in that area. Some persons among them are fed much better than others, and some are poorly nourished. A few of them get hold of so much food that they eat to excess and keep extra amounts in storage for later personal use, some of which may rot with the passage of time. Since the whole group, especially the mass of less nourished ones, pay much respect and honor to those who are fed well, there exists in the compound an incentive for the people to eat well and become strong rather than to share the food with others. Even the ones who hurt themselves with obesity and other complications of eating too much feel that as long as they are big and well fed they are not going to be bothered or harassed by the other strong ones of the group as much as the weak individuals who do not get their fair share, nor can they defend themselves well.

The inequality of the supply of food among those individuals is not necessarily proportional to their degree of hard work for the compound, nor directly related to their human qualities and their need for the food. Some of them devise clever ways of getting hold of more food which would correctly be the portion of others, or they may encourage many less nourished individuals by amusing them, stimulating their sympathy, deceiving them, or simply cheating them with false promises, to give up and donate to these people part of their own supply. Through this vicious cycle of the stronger persons oppressing the weaker and managing to receive continuously part of their food together with much of their support and respect, the nutrition gap becomes wider rather than corrected and reduced. Even on the occasions that a stronger person takes away by force the food from the weak hand of one who is feeble, the group may at times look the other way and try not to get involved. A few among them spend much effort in calculating the number of calories of food which is left for the less fortunate ones, trying to divide it among them in some way that may improve their health and chance for survival. They may even help with the use of their figures and adjustments, in better choice of the types of crops they grow and more appropriate use of the soil in the garden.

They are all ignoring the fact that they would neither have the need for such difficult manipulations of the numbers related to the food supply nor the necessity of the struggle with any shortage of it if they paid proper attention to their real problem. They can perhaps all feel the pleasure of receiving even more than sufficient nourishment:

- if they change the way they perform,
- if they cooperate in using the farm which is at their disposal, with the garden being only a corner thereof,
- if they cultivate the whole farm that is much more than sufficient for their needs, but is partly used by some of their people for games and other recreation or amusement, and much of it completely wasted and covered by weeds.

They are actually concentrating their attention on the small garden which is used to such an extent that they do not see their big farm and its potential for proper use. They have difficulty in controlling some of their people who misbehave by causing damage to the garden or wasting a portion of the available food due to carelessness or through selfish acts and even destroying much of the ingredients of the food through their games and play. They cannot imagine with optimism having the cooperation of the large family needed for making proper use of the whole farm.

Instead of their having repeated discussions on what kinds of serious problems exist in their garden or related to the storage of the food, they ought to get their acts properly together, orchestrating ways of helping the ones who are willing to assist in better use of the farm and unselfish support of the whole group, at the same time strongly opposing the destructive or wasteful acts of their selfish peers. They do not all realize that through persistence in right actions, the appropriate use of the whole farm adequately, the proper division of large quantity of their harvest and abundant meat produced through their cooperative effort, which work can become fun and pleasure when they become accustomed to it, they may have an extra supply available for everybody to the point that they would not need to worry continuously about food. Then, they could probably enjoy life and do what may bring true pleasures without persistent concern about the amount of food and the struggle for their survival, knowing that there can be much supply available, with each grown up person generally feeling and presenting more concern about the nutrition of the whole group and less worry for nourishment of self.

Perhaps some example of their eating and supply of food can apply to parts of our society in regard to its economy and financial resources when paying attention to the magnitude of waste and abuse of human and other resources which are available to the society. Trying to guarantee the satisfactory economic status of our society and future financial stability or comfort of our people, the society should devise ways of supporting the individuals who are trying to do what logically is expected to be beneficial for the future of the society and effectively discourage everybody from being engaged in doing what is in the long run harming the true productivity, economic well-being, and overall financial contentment and happiness of mankind on earth. We should have our eyes open with proper appreciation of what goes on around us. Then as members of the society, we should have the tendency of giving privileges and support, as mentioned repeatedly in this book, to better and more decent people, for the good that they are trying to do and not for their wealth or other worldly power.

In a basic calculation of the subject of our economy, it is important to pay attention to the positive and negative points of our society's productivity. No matter how we play with the income tax game and how the governments try to manipulate it, it is not possible that tax adjustments per se can solve all of the problems of our economy, since, after all, that is just shifting the money or the shortage of it between different parts of the society. The government and the people are all parts of the same society. What is important is the collective wealth of the whole society and, of course, the continuation of production of this wealth as it is being used up at the same time. It is the balance between productivity in general and the overall consumption of this great asset, or the result of subtracting our negatives all over the world from the positives everywhere, that determines how well the society of mankind with a constant population is performing financially, which figure may then affect all of us in some way.

From the point of view of productivity, I categorize the actions of people into three groups: the pluses, the ineffectives, and the minuses.

-The pluses result in production of materials and services which are beneficial towards longer lasting and more comfortable life of the society and the well-being of the future of our world, or the services which are supportive as they would directly or indirectly enhance the above products and their usefulness.

-The minuses are somehow resulting in reduction of the total value of ongoing happiness and comfort in the society, directly or indirectly causing future increase of sadness and discomfort, or they prevent, neutralize, or reduce the efficacy of any of the aforementioned pluses.

-The ineffectives are actions which have neither beneficial nor detrimental effect on the future contentment of the society, although some of these can be grouped together with the minuses if they are wasting the valuable time of some productive members of the society who could be otherwise helping to increase the positive values.

There are many businesses and industries which are productive, clearly improving the economy of the society. There are, at the same time, many with a wide range of success, regarding their performance and financial growth, which have, in my calculations, parasitic function, as they owe their survival or apparent achievements to the productivity and decent work of others while in the long run they are, in a selfish and unfair manner, knowingly causing direct or indirect harm to the whole society's future well-being, happiness and financial stability.

There are many people who are truly productive in a very honest way, being valuable assets for our society. Yet, I personally do not consider all working people as pluses for the society. I prefer to pay attention to the final result of their work and intention. The farmers with their family performing hard mental and physical work may produce our food while they are exposed to many professional hazards. But, if some farmers are engaged in cultivation of what is useless or possibly harmful, they are definitely not included among the pluses. The hard working people of society who are producing and manufacturing what is necessary for our sustenance and comfort are valuable pluses, but the ones whose intentions and efforts result in the production of what is detrimental to the well-being of the society and its future, even if they are paying large sums of money as taxes to the governments and are offering employment with adequate stipend to many in their employ, I consider the outcome of their actions, including the whole mass of human and other assets involved with their work wasted and as negative points when considering the final result of what they do and its effect on our society.

People who are engaged in the distribution and sale of different products can also be considered as positive or negative assets towards the economic status and health of our society when we properly look at the final outcome of their efforts. How could we compare the truck that carries fruit to a market with a truck that is distributing alcoholic beverages? Can we compare the work of a person who sells items of gambling to the casinos with the one who supplies students with their school necessities? May we compare the result of the efforts of the ones who are involved in the production and sale of scientific books with the ones occupied in supplying the society with books and magazines that contain pictures with indecent exposures and untrue demoralizing writings or stories?

The results of what we do, whether beneficial or detrimental to the society, can be considered as positive and negative points for the collective effect on the well-being of the society, financial and otherwise. Among us, a wide variety of behaviors can be observed in this regard.

There are teachers who struggle to educate the ones in need of learning. They insist on sharing their knowledge with the society, educating future generations to be truly productive. There are people of different trades, professions or other work who are conscientiously spending their efforts in trying to perform their duties close to the best of their ability in the way of serving the society. There are others who try very hard, using their talent and intelligence, to find ways to make money without any productivity. Some search for clever excuses so that they are unjustifiably confirmed to have a disability. Some make false promises through nonexistent businesses. Some devise techniques of accusing others unfairly of wrongdoing, then making them pay large sums of money. Some make part of their fortune through formation of a corporation and then declaring its bankruptcy. Some may offer useless telephone or other conversations, wasting people's time while securing their own income. Some look for a good excuse, or make one, to have enough reason for filing a claim against any other individual or organization, in the way of earning something.

There are individuals busy with tremendous financial involvement in the manufacture, distribution and sale of products such as tobacco, alcoholic beverages, or other addictive substances. While the society can see the injuries from such materials and the sick suffer from complications of their use, we may observe advertisements targeting and encouraging new victims to become users.

The price that our society is paying for acts of the criminals is tremendous. They cause, in many ways, serious damage. The robbers, who are taking away in large and small quantities what has been earned by productive people, not only are the source of that direct loss for the society, but also cause other harms, such as the emotional outcome resulting in damage to people's productivity and waste of their time or money and effort spent often in the struggle to prevent future robberies. Needless to say, these and other crimes and criminals cause much loss to the society in many different ways. The criminal, for a very short-lasting selfishness, causes damages which are often long-lasting, irreversible and unforgettable. The society also has to spend enormous amounts of resources towards other provisions because of these criminals, such as the facilities and personnel for incarceration and punishment, the great expense for maintenance of an adequately strong and equipped police force, and the total manpower needed for having courts of justice in operation, causing the involvement of many lawyers on both sides of the debates, with judges and members of juries all spending times which could be used elsewhere in the service of the society.

If there exist some judges who fail to serve proper justice towards the criminals because of fear for their own safety or concern for their future popularity or the vote and their re-election, I consider them as negative points towards securing the society's economic stability, as are any attorneys who knowingly try to cover the guilt of criminals, presenting them as not guilty to others because of personal prestige and financial or other gains, helping the guilty ones escape proper justice.

26

Children, Family, and our Economy

Teachers, in any nation or whatever part of our world, have, I believe, much effect on the economy of our society. Depending on the quality of their work, they may influence the future well-being of a society as very strong pluses or down to serious minuses. One excellent teacher may be the cause of fantastic qualities in many of the members of our younger generation, resulting in a tremendous amount of positive values offered by each of those students to the society later in life. At the same time, one teacher who may be the source of harmful education due to ignorance, carelessness, or possession of devious qualities and character, may divert many young ones from the right path, causing the society of the future to suffer losses due to deficiencies present in each of those individuals. Every nation and any part of its society ought to pay considerable attention and provide strong support to the system of education, the schools, the libraries and related places and institutions. They should spend effort in the selection of properly qualified educators with wonderful human qualities and adequate willingness and ability for teaching. Then they should support them, financially and otherwise, and try to help them do their best in supplying learning minds of our society with the right material.

Education has the utmost influence on the future finances and other strengths of our society. We all should try to be interested in education, which is not secluded to the interior of school buildings, nor does it start at any particular age. Perhaps it should begin with the birth of the child, or somehow even before the birth. If we take into consideration the parents' preparation of themselves and their surroundings for the future baby's physical and emotional requirements, then we realize that in some ways education may start before the beginning of the pregnancy. We must encourage the children and younger generation to develop the love of reading, studying and learning. Yet, education is not only the learning of how to read and write or the subjects of science, but the vast variety of what one is to be educated on, in preparation for the life ahead. They should be taught what is appropriate at the proper age.

Through correct education, by those concerned and qualified for this purpose, the youth of our generation may become prepared for helping in the construction of a better society of the future, while they learn what can be needed for success in fulfilling their later responsibilities. They should learn:

- to be thirsty for knowledge, trying to find correct answers to their questions and to strive to know more and more in the way of satisfying their thirst of curiosities in this world with its endless ocean of what is to be known or discovered.
- the way to study, to search, to research, and to learn more.
- to be good for the society and to do to others what they expect others to do to them.
- to be decent, the boys trying to become gentlemen, the girls growing up to be ladies.
- the ways of becoming, according to their capabilities, useful and productive for all, being engaged in the performance of their duties towards helping the society in general, rather than hurting other people for their own gains.
- to be humble, polite, and nice to others.
- to be in control of their emotions when it is right, and to be able to forgive when it is appropriate.
- to have proper principles in life, to live and behave accordingly, and to stand by those principles with courage.
- to be brave in expressing their true opinions, being always concerned to satisfy God Almighty, rather than changing their behavior or principles, against their belief, for the sake of pleasing others.
- to enjoy helping another person learn what is right.

- to be tough, showing their endurance, when it is needed to do so, and to be gentle when it is proper to be so.
- never to give up hope during their difficulties and never to forget their weaknesses at a time of great success.
- to do what is right even if not easy, and to keep from wrongdoing even when they feel the temptation for doing it.
- to enjoy, at the time of leisure, the hobbies and recreation which are in accord with better functioning of their mind and body, rather than only entertainments which are mostly wasteful of their valuable time and what is known to be harmful or the source of promotion of wrongdoing.
- to be pleased with doing good for others, trying to avoid selfishness, greed, and prejudice.
- to be careful in selecting their friends, trying to socialize with better people, avoiding, as much as possible, the influential association of those who are accustomed to doing wrong.

The process of education of children and young ones may be challenging and at times difficult, but if approached with a sense of responsibility and dedication, it can become fun, interesting, and wonderfully rewarding. We have to try very hard to perform this delicate task correctly. Then, after having spent the needed effort in what we feel is the right direction and having made the sacrifices which are probably necessary towards fulfilling such an important responsibility, if the result is suitable to our desire we ought to be appreciative; if the outcome does not favorably meet our expectations we should try to accept gracefully what we cannot control or change, yet be content with our conscience for having tried our part.

It is very important, if at all possible, that children live with or very close to both of their parents during their growing years, and when the very young one is at home, at least one parent should be generally available, providing the sweet atmosphere of home education. People who take the responsibility of childbearing ought to try very hard to continue the duty of parenthood with preparation of useful family life, so that the children receive, as well as possible from both parents, the optimal ingredients which are required for their adequate physical, mental and behavioral maturation towards becoming better members of their future society. Some parents enjoy spending their time with dedication to educating the children correctly. They are pleased with their effort, especially when achieving satisfactory results. Some parents give in to problems or difficulties, leaving this very important responsibility incomplete. They are either themselves lacking the qualities necessary for being proper parents and educators, or they fail in holding to their principles and surrender to peer pressure, leaving their children to grow up more and more devious, adapting to misbehaviors of the ones they socialize with from the wrong section of the society.

When the attitude of these youngsters becomes more crooked, there can be steep escalation of the degree of difficulty for their parents in being able to aid them effectively or save them from their downfall. Perhaps it is much more practical to try to keep the children from approaching the cliff when they are starting to divert from the right path. If they start to fall, saving them can prove to be more and more difficult as they fall deeper and are trapped by the many vices which may be accompanied by strong temptations at that age. Then the parents who notice their children's misery regret not having spent the needed small fraction of that effort at the proper time to guide them in the right way. The parent's desire for the children's receiving the right education may not be enough, as it is important to have the availability of committed parents to supply that education.

In the same way that in other organizations we have individuals assigned to their responsibilities or duties, there should be the tendency towards having one of the two spouses as the main supplier of the income or earning what is needed for the sustenance of the family and having the authority or being in charge of making the final decisions related to the performance of the family unit, of course, with needed consultations among the members. The other spouse should be in the position of being in close touch with their children at the residence and able to put together what is necessary for preparation of a sweet home environment for all. For the parents' success in doing better for their children and for themselves, there should be somehow an orderly division of responsibilities with differences in the performance so that the two individuals of opposite gender appreciate the mutual need for their cooperation, each of them having the healthy feeling of incompleteness without the other one.

If the two spouses keep being different from each other in their physical appearance or outfit, in their emotional or behavioral characteristics towards the family and the society, in their responsibilities at home and outside, this should not be the cause for alarm and struggle in claiming equality. We can be different, as we are, and continue to enjoy our differences while perhaps feeling a stronger bond together and more need for one another in the same way that the pumping work of a heart and the gas exchange capacity of the lung are both necessary in the body. Though the responsibilities are so different, actions on the part of both are necessary, and there is no need to compare or try to establish superior or inferior degrees of importance. The functions of both should be considered indispensable. With their appropriate differences, the two spouses are going to be in need of one another and attached together more than if each claims self-sufficiency with the capability of carrying out both jobs well, independent of the other spouse.

Although marriage is a contractual arrangement, it is not right that, in trying to make it successful and long-lasting, the society place difficulties for the process of separation and divorce, as this may generate fear in the mind of the youth of either gender of ever getting married. The joining with commitments of the two persons of the opposite gender, for the purpose of formation of a family unit, should not only be as a legal and social contract, but also be reinforced with the two of them feeling their mutual attachment to one another with other more permanent or long-lasting factors. The functional need is important, as the two of them keep their differences in responsibilities at home and in the society for better achievements, or to complement each other's performance as a combined unit or team. The emotional, sentimental or affectionate attachment of their persons is perhaps a much more necessary factor, so that they remain in need of one another by strengthening this adherence, even if the other material needs, such as the bonds related to financial status or social function, disappear and the affinities related to the body and physical characteristics are diminished with the passage of time.

Another important factor worthy of serious consideration is parents' intimacy with others in the society, such as relatives or friends, who help with good intentions in reinforcing the family unit. It is perhaps equally important that the laws and rules related to dissolution of the marriage do not make it easy for one spouse to gain a very comfortable life through divorce by taking advantage of the other one's hard work, so that a person does not marry with the intention of gaining future security by taking away a portion of another person's financial and other means of livelihood. This may better guarantee the sincere mutual need of the spouses for one another, with or without children, and can perhaps greatly reduce the rate of divorce in some communities.

If, in the society, adequate effort is not made to prepare the means for encouraging the formation and continuation of a healthy family life, we may have serious ongoing injury to the economy, health, comfort, happiness, and moral values of our communities and suffer the consequence of a powerful and viciously destructive circle. This circle is formed as a chain with many interrelated rings, such as:

- Lack of a decent family life.
- The future of children and their growth influenced by their deficiency in receiving needed affection and proper education. As a result having youngsters with a multitude of complexes, since their physical, mental, and emotional training can be influenced by their life on the streets with wrong companions, away from home or at home, occupied by useless entertainments and being lonely while both parents are busy elsewhere.
- The availability of addictive substances.
- Promiscuity with its serious physical and emotional complications.
- The birth of children out of wedlock.
- The involvement of people of different ages, as individuals or as groups, in major vices or criminal activities.
- The lack of trust or confidence among friends or relatives.
- And as a result, more instability of the foundations for construction and maintenance of a proper family life, causing further serious damage to the future well-being, productivity, and economy of our society.

27

Service or Disservice

People who are in positions of higher authority, such as members of government in a country and elected or appointed officials in different parts of the world, capable of influencing the life of an important section of any nation or community through their performance, can be considered as important pluses or minuses towards the economic well-being of a society. The actions of each of these individuals can also be divided into different categories, since each person may generate a variety of what can have positive or negative effects towards our society's financial stability. There are some who endure self-sacrifices and hardship for the sake of the comfort or well-being of others, and there are some who hurt many through what they do for the sake of their own pleasure or the satisfaction of the few who are favored by them.

There are those who believe it is a valuable occasion to be in that responsible situation, and they try very hard to do much good for the society during their time, and there are the ones who feel it is an opportunity to be capable of taking advantage of what is at their disposal for a period of time, and they do as much as possible to guarantee their own future comfort or to secure their position for a long time, inconsiderate of the damage done to others. There are those who consider their position with its responsibilities an opportunity for serving the society while they continue to be humble and nice to others. There are also others who use their authority as an occasion for being able to manifest arrogance and superiority towards the average members of the society, although it is the collective force of the same people that they use as the support to sustain their authority, and perhaps among those people are the ones who elected them to their positions of power.

The decisions and actions of influential persons can affect the lives and performance of a number of other people, with beneficial and detrimental outcomes as a result, influencing the productivity and the economic status of the society. It is not right that some of us offer much respect with support to people of influence, inconsiderate of their personal qualities and the true value of their intentions and actions. In the same way it is not fair if some of us stereotype that category of individuals as being corrupt. Although the excess of power and the abundance of wealth in this world can have strong corruptive effect that many of us may not be able to resist, there are many wonderful people who have much of either or both, yet they keep from being influenced by the temptations for the abuse of these worldly luxuries. While these individuals spend much of their efforts truly serving their communities and the whole society, they view their money and power as temporary means in this world to give them the ability to serve others more effectively.

It is up to us the members of the society to strive towards dealing with authoritative people more appropriately according to their goodwill, or what we consider to be their intention for true service to the society, rather than their mere financial or other capabilities. We should pay attention to what good they do, rather than how well they speak about their own performance. We have to try as well as we can, in judging with our wisdom their true character and intentions, rather than having our sentiments influenced by how nicely they play with words, how well they afford to advertise and how strongly the news media portrays their favorable or unfavorable character for us. In other words, we should try very hard to control our emotions so that we are not manipulated by their appearance and their words, nor by the news media and advertisements, but judging them wisely by what we feel they really intend and are capable of doing in their capacity for long-lasting financial and other well-being of the society. Otherwise, we may support more and more those who know how to look after their own economic status, even if they are not the right ones for helping to secure a better economy and future comfort for the whole society.

In relation to politics and elected officials, I believe another financial waste for the society is the money together with the manpower spent for different political campaigns and activities in excess of what would be the basic presentation of necessary but simple facts to the public and the ones who vote or make the selections.

28

Competitions, and Economy

In many aspects of our social life we are wasting excessive amounts of our time and resources in useless competitions, above the basic level which is required for keeping incentives for better performance. Instead of cooperating with friendly competitions to excel our function, there are many who present dislike, negative propaganda and by chance acts of harm or violence against one another in their competition. The resulting loss can be little or great. There are the ones who use aggression or hateful behavior in competitions related to sports. There are immoral or at times illegal actions taken by competitors who are engaged in trade or manufacturing of products or the ones who offer professional or other services. They may use negative remarks about one another, or they cause trouble for each other.

On a much larger scale we may view competition for political influence and the struggle for power of different nations of our world and the tremendous volume of human and financial resources spent on preparation for showing the force of defense or aggression and then the use of it with related destructions and their long-lasting later effects, as very serious economic losses for our society. This would be unnecessary if the people of the world lived, as we are supposed to, with proper appreciation of this beautiful planet and the life on it. I cannot be very optimistic in feeling or anticipating that the future generations of mankind would get to mix together in different nations and countries with friendly relations to the point that the governments, or better to say some of the people as government officials or in other capacities, who generate or augment, for the sake of security of their own positions, hatred among the nations, will not be able to change those people's friendship to enmity.

I have my doubts because even in any one country or a small community at times we see the behavior of extremists or the unfriendly and illogical actions of groups against each other. After all, the nations and countries are formed with larger groups of the same kind of people, and it is the same behavior that can be observed, but on a larger scale. Still, I want to believe that hopefully the people of our future generations become better educated, behave more rationally, live more wisely, and even in their competitions treat each other more appropriately. They shall become cognizant of the fact that through constructive cooperation with one another, as individuals or as whatever size masses and groups, they can all benefit from satisfactory results and that by causing damage to each other's performance or achievements while competing at whatever level, although at a given moment there may be the feeling of success for being ahead of some others, the negative values will ultimately affect the overall collective joy of the society which they and their dear ones are members thereof.

Some during their struggle for survival in this world, instead of using a group cooperation to make it more harmonious with better chance for all, compete, living at the expense of possible damage to the quality of life of others. In this competition they have become selfish, with their mind concentrating on the quantity of worldly treasures they can control, to the point that they devise ways of making money through useless activities or doing what can directly or indirectly be harmful to the life and future of others. This causes damage of the highest magnitude to the economy of our society.

Without mentioning a particular example, may I remind you of the persons generally occupied in a variety of businesses, whether manufacturing and distributing products or offering services, who intentionally bring down the quality of their service or product in their efforts to make it more profitable, disregarding the damage done to the economy of others and the whole society through their actions. Many other people may be engaged in doing the work which is totally useless or clearly harmful to our society and its future. Some of these individuals may succeed, through their selfish and harmful acts, in getting hold of much wealth, fame, recognition, and power. It is, at the same time, very sad that we, as the members of this very society which is hurt through their actions, offer to them our respect which they do not deserve and our support that encourages them to continue their vicious activities.

Now, as a particular example, may I mention that perhaps some of the people in entertainment industry, in the way of competing for higher popularity of their products, whether producing movie or magazine or television programs and talk shows, at times disregard their social responsibilities or human values and present what is prone to be socially injurious and morally devious to our young and old.

This they do in competition with their benevolent colleagues, instead of joining them in the proper use of these powerful means of information to which they have access for positive service with adequate attempt at educating others with the right material and presenting what can promote the society's well-being, productivity, total happiness, and future economic stability, rather than their own temporary gains while hurting even the useful performance of the ones they compete with. They may bring the wrong but attractive scenes to our view or intentionally give us interesting but misguiding news and information. They may present without shame sexually deviated individuals, the persons with indecent outfit or behavior, and the ones accustomed to criminal acts or addicted to serious wrongdoing, as normal individuals in ordinary touch with the society, or use them as figures of entertainment, encouraging the society to tolerate them, getting used to their misconduct, or they present them as examples of achievement or success, making them heroes and role models.

Perhaps in this country alone, if we try to eliminate the deleterious actions that we take in our competition for survival and the great waste of the society's time and efforts by destructive forces that we are using against each other, we may live with almost heavenly pleasures. If this spirit of cooperation and assistance, rather than selfish concerns, is practiced amongst the different countries, we would see that, with so much of the resources at our disposal on this planet and the abundance of the blessings bestowed upon us by Our Creator, most of the people on earth could be adequately provided for and comfortable in this life.

While trying to climb the mountain of achievements and successes in this world, different attitudes can be observed among the people. Some, in the process of competing to get to the top, keep pushing others down. Then when they get higher they are lonely while at the same time continuously worried about the time of decline. Some, while trying to go up, keep helping others climb as well, then the higher they go, while enjoying a better view of life, the more pleasure they get out of sharing the view with others. Since these individuals are pleased with the appreciation of happiness of others, they are not worried about their time of descent. They feel that whenever they come down they can be happy wholeheartedly, knowing that others, some of whom they have assisted, will be up there enjoying the view while all of the other nice people, whether on or off the mountain, continue to enjoy the pleasure of sharing.

How could anybody deny that our having or lacking the attitude of cooperation among us has tremendous effect on our economy? If we all try to be less selfish, improving the quality of what we do and assisting others in doing better, being concerned about the future of all and not only our own, we may get to the point of providing an abundance of the materials of this world for the whole society to the point of not needing to worry about the problems related to economy. If it is true that the manufacturers of some of the products at the present time in our society intentionally keep from producing their best quality of long-lasting materials because of the fear of reducing the need for parts, repairs and replacements, this would be a wrong attitude according to my simple understanding. The making of their best quality and longest-lasting of what are the necessities for the society's comfortable life would be ultimately a plus in helping the economy.

It is not how high a percentage of people are employed and how hard they work that guarantee the financial contentment of the people and the economic well-being of the society, but how well the average members of this society are and continue to be supplied with their needs for basic happiness and comfort. If the necessity of making new products is less, and through better quality of work and performance fewer hours of work suffice, then as long as the society is supplied better with an abundance of necessities, there is going to be availability of manpower to do other productive work. Fewer hours of work will be needed for each person. There would be fewer traffic jams and other stressful problems to be faced with. More parents can stay at home with their children rather than having to work, and the ones who are the out-of-home working force may have much more time to spend with their family or at other activities.

As long as the reduction of the need for work is accompanied by abundance of products of better quality and availability of our basic necessities there would be not only less work needed on average for each individual but also lower prices for goods and at the same time better quality of life for the society, since there is more comfort and less stress by having better products to deal with at home and outside:

- When our cars, machinery, light bulbs, tools or equipment, the surface of our roads, and the parts of our buildings last longer, without need for repairs or replacement.
- When we have fewer people participating in parasitic businesses, which are perhaps more concentrated in the urban areas, and they get out to do real, productive work.
- When unimaginably large quantities of money and other resources are saved through better performance and less waste.
- When we are not involved in deceiving or hurting one another in different ways.

Then, in spite of each person, on average, needing to do less work and face less stress, there would be an increase in the total value of the effort spent to secure an adequate supply of what are the essential requirements for the society's lasting comfort and happiness. This increase in the supply of what we all need can help to eliminate the poverty and reduce the financial gap in the society. At the same time, in such a society there would be diminution of incentive for anyone's struggle in making and keeping an excessive amount of wealth. This society of people does not honor its individuals, nor offer them extra favor, merely because of the abundance of their worldly treasures. In fact the persistent excessive wealth, by itself, could be a cause for reduction of its owner's social popularity and respect. This society is well-supplied with what would be required for everybody's comfort. This society with its individuals is not eager to collect and save to excess, as each person would be more anxious to comfort others and feels confident towards receiving sincere care from others whenever required. And finally this society's members would have the will, the means and the time for helping each other while in constant competition doing more good for one another rather than being concerned about the security of self alone.

29

'Economy in 'Health, Sickness, and 'Death

In every country or organized nation a very large part of the finances is spent on health care. At the present state of our civilization much of this enormous budget is being wasted, causing a serious and detrimental blow to the economy of our society. We can identify a variety of factors with potential influence on this important loss. Much of this waste is the result of our society's lifestyle with repeated mistakes which are directly or indirectly damaging our health. Unethical, undisciplined sexual practices in any community can be the source of a multitude of costly health problems. The sexually transmitted diseases, the diverse issues in connection with unwanted pregnancies, the abortions without medical indication, the battered babies or the illnesses of babies and children who are left with inadequate care or supervision, and the crimes committed in relation to promiscuity, are all causing great economic loss. There must be, at the same time, perhaps a greater loss because the ones involved with these problems can have much difficulty with appropriate use of the valuable time of productivity, whether as a student in college, a parent at home, or a person with responsibilities at work.

Another phenomenon that results in tremendous waste of our health budget is the abuse of alcohol and other addictive substances with the resultant variety of diseases and injuries or related crimes, as repeatedly referred to elsewhere in this book. At the same time, there may be waste of the budget through the large volume of trauma and costly injuries due to careless, selfish, aggressive, and at times criminal actions of some people without the influence of alcohol or other like substances. There can be a very appreciable cost in relation to health problems as a result of our defaults in self-care and hygiene or the incorrect use of what can be in the right amounts necessary or physiological, for example, the excessive exposure to the ultraviolet light with the resultant cancers of skin, and the problem of overeating with the vast variety of due complications as a serious burden to the health of some parts of our society.

There is also great waste of our health budget and other resources of the society because of the physical and emotional complications of stress. This stress that many members of our society suffer from is in relation to the few examples of health problems mentioned above and to other serious deficiencies in our society's present lifestyle, as we do not do what we are supposed to do, as we do what we are not to, and as we cause hurt to one another partly being selfish and partly through ignorance or carelessness. It seems that much of what is spent nowadays for health care in many communities is somehow misplaced or is lacking a reasonable order of priorities. Logically, perhaps we could spend more towards education, research, and other means related to prevention of diseases. We could spend more on making our environment a healthier place to live in, from both physical and mental points of view. We could spend more on our efforts to eradicate or eliminate everywhere a variety of factors that we can identify, without need for a microscope, as agents causing damage to the health of our society and people.

On the other hand, we could lessen inhumane expenses by reducing our efforts to elongate the misery or suffering of a person who is terminally ill against the will of that person. We could spend less in costly treatments and procedures which do not offer worthwhile improvement of quality of life for our people, but are prone to make the last part of their lives more difficult instead of letting them go through the natural process of dying with dignity. Our society should realize that there is a time for leaving us to die without having in our way too much of costly interference that could be spent towards the health care of the ones who might have long and better lives ahead. We could also try to prioritize the expenditures related to health care, with the tendency towards spending more for the care of innocent patients rather than those who are ill due to their own wrongdoing and guilt.

Another serious misplacement of what is spent on health care, though unrelated to incorrect selection of what we spend it on, is certainly related to where the money goes, which problem can severely increase the waste of the budget at the same time that it seriously lowers the quality of health care of our society. There are many conscientious individuals in professions related to health care, treating others as well as they expect to be treated by others, but our society can be seriously hurt:

- If there are some who generate much unnecessary expense for their communities through their selfish intentions.

- If there are some hospitals, insurance companies, or other institutions connected to the medical profession with particular interest in making profit, more than their concern about the quality of the service they offer to their patients, even to the point that through their squeezing of the pockets of people with insufficient resources, they may generate so much capital gains that they would need to find ways of spending much of it in unnecessary projects to avoid tax or other obligations.

- If there are some physicians and surgeons whose main objective at work is self-satisfaction through personal financial and other gain rather than offering appropriate care and education to their community, and if they may perform tests and treatments or surgical procedures with the objective of some benefit for themselves rather than the best indication for their patients, or that they try to get as much money as possible from people who can afford it and the ones who cannot afford it.

- If there are some non-medical personnel in administrative work or the medical professionals who have become solely engaged in management of the financial aspect of medical work, with the main intention of making money while they cause hurt and make life difficult for both the provider and the receiver of medical services. (They may make large profit that they do not deserve as they oppress their community, and while they can seriously damage the quality of medical care, they stabilize their own position. Then with the help of their undeserving wealth and power they may acquire the respect and support of the same community that they have hurt.)

- If there are pharmacists or others involved in the production, distribution and sale of medications or other products needed for the health care of our society, whose efforts in profit-making may cause the items which are produced at reasonable cost to be sold at unfairly high prices. (Some patients who deserve medical care may not succeed in receiving the proper treatment nor afford to have access to the medication or supply that they need while large volumes of supplies, services, and expertise are being wasted, left without use or abused.)

Another problem related to health care that can cause serious damage to the economy of our society is some people's abuse of the legal system in the process of controlling the quality of service. I believe the abuse of the legal profession may damage many aspects of our lives, but its involvement with the medical practice can result in noticeably greater detrimental effect. We could perhaps blame different groups of our people with different degrees of fault or guilt for causing or augmenting this problem. There may be some in the practice of medicine who are generating much distrust in their communities due to their poor performance. They may apply their profession, which is supposed to be honorably in the service of others, as a careless business resulting in undue injuries through their negligence, receiving blame that they deserve, making the society lose the needed confidence even towards the other decent members of their profession. There may be some patients or their beneficiaries who make claims against the professionals in the interest of some gain when they find an excuse to do so, even if at the time they do not believe in anybody's guilt or negligence. There may be some lawyers who stimulate distrust when they sabotage the rapport between the medical practitioners and their patients with false accusation of a nonexistent guilt or fault, with the intention of profit for self.

All of this can be a source of economic loss for the society. This loss is partly a direct result of hurting the financial status of many involved. At the same time, there can be a very important financial loss caused indirectly through the wasting of the valuable time of many productive people or by causing injury to the needed confidence and rapport in the practice of the medical profession, resulting in damage to the quality of its performance, or through disturbing the people's peace of mind which is required for the proper function of our society. While availability of adequate legal support with its application at the right time is needed, the abuse of this powerful tool in relation to medical practice as well as other professions or businesses can inflict serious injury on the economy of any community, possibly making some dishonest individuals wealthy, some innocents poor, and a great many people stressed unnecessarily.

After people die, the time, efforts, and resources that we spend to discard the body, in excess of what is needed for this simple process, can be considered an economic loss for our communities. We should try to comfort the members of our society, spending for them as they deserve while they are living. Once they are gone, it is perhaps our spiritual support and prayers that may help them. The unnecessary expenses for the quality of the coffin or purchase of a permanent resting ground or beautification of the corpse or spending on the related extravagant ceremonies can all be considered as loss of the society's assets with no useful worldly or other-worldly outcome. What luxury we add to the procedure of taking care of the dead body is not for helping the separated soul but to please or comfort ourselves. It seems to me as if through these acts we try to change the outlook of death in an effort to reduce our fear of it. But this would be fooling ourselves, since correctly we should educate our young and old not to be greatly concerned about the moment of dying and what happens to the body, but to try to look beyond that instant.

We ought to have our pleasure and fear in relation to what we expect to feel in our permanent lives and not confuse ourselves by paying much attention to wasted material luxury at the moment of our separation from this world. If we correctly understand this fact, then during our lives on earth we should live right and do what is proper, with serious concern about what we are going to get, not materially at the time of death, but after having gone through that phase. When we approach a door which is opening, it is not the decoration on the door that we are concerned about, but the place that we are entering and what we are going to get in that place, whether it is a well–supplied, beautiful garden or the unpleasant atmosphere of a prison. With this in mind and through this logical reasoning one would strive in doing good and looking forward to the moment of death with hope and expectation for what comes beyond that period. Then any expected potential difficulty related to death can become not only tolerable but welcomed. In the same way, one who is pregnant can be anxiously looking forward to the moment of labor, when expecting the pleasant excitement of motherhood to follow.

30

Living on Earth and Searching in Space

The availability and continuation of supply of what are the necessities for our people's proper contentment in this life are an important indicator of our society's economic strength. At the same time, we have to keep in mind that the degree of adequacy is not only according to the volume of supply, but also dependent on the need or the quantity of consumption. We should spend cooperative effort everywhere towards improving our productivity, reducing our wasteful and destructive acts, and correcting the imperfections of our lifestyles, to increase the supply of what we need. But for maintaining the average adequacy of the people's financial contentment we should also pay attention to the volume or mass of the population consuming the available resources all over the world.

We need to search for ways to offer proper encouragement and incentives for control of population of the world in general and also of the big cities and urban areas. This must be done to reduce the multitude of problems related to overcrowding in each society. The population control of our world should not be achieved through unwise wars, cruel criminal abortions and unnecessary waves of famine or epidemic diseases, which cause miseries and result in stress affecting the minds and lives of the ones involved and of many others close by or faraway, but through proper ways of family planning, with correct techniques of contraception and with abstinence from promiscuity. I have a strong feeling that the reason that some religious groups oppose birth control may be due to previous misinterpretation of instructions. It is time that religious leaders and scholars make adequate effort to study the truth and to correct existing misunderstandings.

The other possibility is that some groups in the past had the belief that through uncontrolled reproduction their increase in number may help them meet triumphs. This selfish view may be corrected if we people of the world strive to unite in friendship, strengthen our decent common goals, and at the same time try very hard to ignore our unimportant differences and get rid of the chronic unfounded prejudice of our groups against each other. In trying to improve the status of life on earth, we should pay attention not only to our population in terms of numbers, but also in terms of quality. In this regard, there could be ways of having more education and encouragement towards effective contraception for the ones with known hereditary mental or physical disorders and the carriers of troublesome genes.

Of the efforts and sums of money spent on the programs and activities related to space discoveries, some are useful towards valuable scientific progress and explorations that can help to improve the condition of life on earth. The other part of the funds which is spent with the intention of finding for the future another place in this world for continuation of human life is a waste. It is totally illogical if, instead of controlling the population and having an optimum number to live happily with the available resources on this planet, we overcrowd this one and try to find extra space elsewhere. It is the quality of life of our society that counts, not the quantity or the vastness of the surface we can occupy. If we cannot clean up our acts and have a decent life here, how can we expect to have a better one elsewhere? Therefore, it is unjustifiable to take our wrongdoings to outer space and try to contaminate or pollute other places as well.

Besides, how could we ever expect to find in this world a place better than the earth, or even as good a place, when this is the most suitable for our material life, since through the progression of our time here we have developed adequate physiological harmony to this surrounding with whatever qualities it has, whether the composition of the air we breathe or the succession of the days and the nights. The surface of the earth is large enough for us to live happily here. We are not to reproduce and multiply to the point that we outgrow this vast surface. This is our perfect home for this life. What we ought to do is to spend much effort to safeguard this planet with the living conditions on it for the suitable number of people in our present generation of mankind and the ones following us, keeping our lives void of wrongdoings and our habitat clean from pollutions.

31

Cost of Being Entertained

What we do for entertainment and how we use our times of leisure can have a very strong effect on the economy of the society. A wide range of possibilities exists in our attitude towards the way we may spend our time in recreation. There are those among us who enjoy being productive. Even in their free time they may get pleasure out of doing what can directly or indirectly help the society. The people of this group choose for their regular occupation the work or profession that is expected to support the economic and other strengths of the society. In their free time these individuals may be occupied with pleasure in carrying out other productive responsibilities. They may take part in the proper education of children. They may be engaged in sport, doing what can improve their physical and mental capabilities towards better performance. They may spend time in the use of their words and actions to encourage and help others to do better. They may try to prepare a sweet and suitable living atmosphere for their family and neighbors and do good in helping friends and strangers. They may build or produce what is useful, or they apply their abilities in any other way that, while they get pleasure out of what they do, the others and ultimately the society may benefit from their efforts.

There are many among us who spend a lot of time being entertained in doing what can be totally useless, and there are some among us who choose for their entertainment what can be detrimental to their own ongoing productivity or what is a source of harm to others and to the society's future well-being. It is very logical to claim that we as a society should try to educate our younger generation from very early childhood to learn how to enjoy doing what is good and how to be pleased with self restraint of temporary desires and abstinence from doing what, according to their judgment, is harmful to themselves or to the society. Then as adults they may continue to be pleased with useful hobbies and entertainment rather than indulging in useless or harmful amusements.

It seems that at present many people in our society, when choosing entertainment, have given up their feeling of responsibility for being wisely selective and have succumbed to their temporary desires, spending a lot of time at useless entertainments, some of which may be very attractive to the point of being almost addictive. They can waste much of their valuable time without even receiving the benefit of becoming refreshed for better future performance in their work. In fact, some entertainments may have double harm, as they not only cause wasting of the time of the productive members of our society, but they also have deleterious effects on their mind and body with indirect injury to their productivity. This negative effect on the society and ultimately on the economy can be tripled when it involves the wasting of time and damaging of the performance of the ones who are in the process of learning, such as the young ones and the students, as the injury caused is not only to their time and the performance at the present work but also to their productivity in the distant future for the society.

In spite of the advancement of our knowledge in science, technology and higher levels of understanding and education by many of our people, we can still observe the spreading and acceleration of involvement of our society with a variety of useless and harmful entertainments. Some responsible authorities may consider the flow of money related to these entertainments as a positive economic marker and the involved working force as a useful support of employment, disregarding the truth that in fact the whole manpower and all of the involved assets are wasted, resulting in strong negative value because of the ultimately serious and detrimental effects on society's future well-being. The owners of industries or places that offer these detrimental entertainments may become wealthier with accelerating speed, showing off with their success in the presence of the very society that they are hurting. Those who support them through the use of harmful entertainments are injured by them. It is as if on this dirty road our short-sighted people are pushing the vehicles of those abusers and helping them advance. Then, once those selfish individuals have advanced with their luxuries they are careless about the same people are left behind, pushing and getting blind and sick while inhaling the dust of the road.

The individuals who are engaged with the presentation to our society of useless and harmful entertainments ought to awaken their conscience, pay attention to the fact that not only the enormous budgets in their control and the work of the ones in their employ are a total waste and create negative value towards the ultimate economic well-being of the society, but they are perhaps causing, directly and indirectly, a multitude of socio-economic problems for decent individuals all over the world. There are a variety of entertainments, activities, hobbies, and habits that may involve the younger generation to the point of ruining the future of many of them, either by occupying much of their valuable time which is supposed to be spent in preparation for a decent life to come or by diverting them from the right productive path, causing tremendous ongoing damage to the economy of the society. Some of the young ones may waste excessive amounts of time in joyful group activities with unsuitable companions, feeling free to proceed with involvement towards promiscuity and with peer encouragement towards dangerous addictions.

Much of this becomes possible with the adult society, whether parents and elders at home or teachers at school, mixing the young ones of the opposite gender together in conditions and an atmosphere that not only prepare the possibility but even promote their wrong involvements. At the same time many of the elders responsible for education may have serious shortcomings in fulfilling their function either due to their weakness against peer pressure in an unsuitable surrounding or due to the deficiencies in their own learning of discipline and understanding.

Some of the places that promote unethical and sinful acts with gambling and indecent entertainment can, in different nations, cause the waste of tremendous volume of human time and other assets of the society. This kind of dangerous entertainment will spread, if not controlled and condemned by the nations with help of religious and ethical beliefs, and may manifest as an epidemic disease or parasite with powerful destructive capabilities, seriously hurting the economy of the productive sector of the society. The sick minds of many individuals affected by this disease may not understand or feel their problem until it is too late for treating its devastating complications.

The publishing and broadcasting industries possess disproportionately high influence through entertainment on the economy of our society. This effect is in both good and bad directions. The better individuals in those industries prepare, through their books and other publications, through the movies and educational films, through their programs in the news media and other means of telecommunication, what can be entertaining to young or old and at the same time helpful towards the betterment of the society. The greedy can through the same means of communication hurt our society with the wrong entertainment and cause enormous damage ultimately to its economy and contentment. They change almost everything into entertainment. They present the seriously unhappy aspects of family life, disturbing the normal behavior and relationships that should exist at home between the young and old and between spouses.

They entertain us by making fun of serious matters of family life. They show repeatedly the indecencies in sexual behavior, as if it is okay for one to have freedom for unclean romance, to use it prior to marriage, and then when married still present romantic behavior towards other than one's own spouse or to stimulate unethical romantic feelings in others. To entertain, they mix almost everything with unclean romance, and to sell their products, they present on almost any occasion the indecently exposed human body. They show indecency of language, outfit, and behavior in the work place, at the school, in the hospital or in other places of the society's function.

They entertain by presenting scenes of crime and violence to the point that they encourage the society to become accustomed to this behavior, and a portion of the society to practice it, too. They bring to us scenes of the court proceedings and trials, some of which may waste much of the time of the society and may even give the wrong message of promoting, rather than discouraging, criminal acts. They present some fiction and stories in the outfit of true happenings, causing confusion in the minds of young and old, by misplacing our feelings and beliefs. They bring to us soap operas, talk shows and similar programs, some of which may contain and present to the public large volumes of what is harmful, causing a tremendous waste of time, misleading young and old, and being detrimental to the future of family and society.

They change the sports from healthy exercises into entertainment, then they encourage a few to practice it and a large portion of the productive force of the society to become almost addicted in spending an appreciable amount of time just watching. They even present some violence or other unethical behavior attached to what is supposed to be sport. They make it more amusing for some viewers who may cheer as crowds, while a few who are as slaves of wealth and other material privileges, fight one another, at times with rage.

They encourage individuals to compete as a way of getting to the top. Some of these competitions can be useless and just for our entertainment, causing the waste of the time of many talented younger individuals. The young are forced, in order to earn fame or finance, into an excessive amount of hard exercise with stress, in doing something to the extent which is in no way productive for the society nor right for each individual's health.

At the competition they present society's expectation that if they do not reach the highest possible positions, they deserve sadness and sense of failure. At times the news people and commentators, some of whom perhaps cannot do much of the same sport but to talk about it, criticize in an unfair manner the hard-working individual with magnificent achievements for a small mistake or for being second or third rather than the very best in the competition. It could be nice if we had the competitions in areas and performances which are useful in the way of encouraging people's productivity for the society, and if we would compete with cooperation, causing an increase of friendship for mankind among the nations of our world.

There are, apparently, in the industries which present the harmful entertainments to society, some individuals functioning who are concerned about their own gains, whether financial or other, but careless about the serious ongoing damage done to the society and its economy. Of course, we as members of this society could be blamed for what goes on, since many of us are spending time and money supporting these productions and encouraging their producers.

After all we are the ones who look for more and more entertainment. We are the ones who expect them to change everything into entertainment for us, whether they be political activities, or the work of professionals such as physicians and judges, or more serious matters such as the religious practices, or even the pictures of disasters, natural and other kinds, or unpleasant scenes of war, crime, famine, and sickness. Many of us may be attracted to these productions more favorably if they are mixed with indecencies, wrongdoings, violence, and a large dose of immoral romance. They are encouraged to present scenes which are supposed to be the very private ingredients and moments of family life and not for public viewing.

For the sake of trying to save the future of our society, the nations of our world should adopt adequate controls over the news media and all of the publishing and broadcasting means except for having freedom of expression of one's opinion. The control may be done through different committees and groups of benevolent professionals of various fields who would be elected in some proper way by the people, the process of election being with a minimum of twisting of the views of the people who vote or select. The members of the monitoring groups and committees should not remain in their positions for too long, so that the nations and people do not lose their adequate control over them, nor would the ones among them who may have a tendency, become corrupted with the continuation of power. I emphasize: as the majority of us can more easily be influenced by our emotions; therefore, it behooves us to permit groups of professionals who are involved in the actual decision-making process to determine what should or should not be presented to the public.

If the mass media would not acquiesce to come under proper control, the distant future of our society can be seriously endangered. I have strong feeling that, other than freedom of speech for expression of opinions, their presentations should be monitored by committees that would have no financial or other personal gainful interest in their product but real concern about the future of our society. Also there should be rules to prevent the possibility that a minority or occasional groups with particular bias would be able to own or manage much of these industries.

Otherwise, if in the distant or near future some people with misguided and selfish intentions manage to take control over a large section of these media in different parts of the world, they may, with the use of their freedom, brain-wash our nations towards their own interests and keep important portions of our society, together with the people's beliefs and actions, under their own control. If that kind of people, void of benevolence, succeed to be in control, they may possibly advocate a variety of moral and other corruptions in the nations and the society, so that people become weak and incapable of realizing what goes on and unable to stand against them. This is because those wrongdoers would know that, properly educated, adequately knowledgeable, decently mannered society with sensible attachment to the religious beliefs and human values or principles cannot be easily manipulated or brain-washed by them. We ought to try very hard to help our younger generation receive proper education at the right time, then as adults they may participate in the formation of a society which is wiser, happier, healthier, and less prone to be misguided.

32

Effect of Negative Productivity on Economy

Another serious and detrimental influence on the society's economy is the availability and abuse of addictives such as drugs, alcohol and tobacco. There should be severe punishment for the illegal dealers of like substances who promote the society's involvement with these addictions. As repeated in this book, it is a terrible miscalculation that the tax money paid by the alcoholic beverage industries, by the gambling houses and casinos, by the manufacturers of tobacco products, by unclean magazines, and by like sources can help the budget of any government. In fact, these kinds of destructive forces undermine the whole well-being, safety, and happiness of the society. They should all be nicely condemned by the people, and the advertisements in their favor banned, so that each community, in the process of competing with the others close by in making money, does not get involved in these destructive activities with the resultant suffering from their moral, social, financial and other serious ill-effects.

Of the people who are very successfully engaged in a variety of businesses and trades, some are busy with the purchase and sale of items or performance of services, which are of no use for the proper function of the society. They may be helping, through their activities, to increase the flow of money, but the time they use on the works of this kind, many of which you may reasonably identify without my being specific in referring to them, is wasted and so are the time and money spent by their customers, since all is of no avail towards productivity or in providing what is needed for the ongoing well-being of the society.

Those who have great financial profits through this type of work may wrongly earn the respect and support of many, but the result of what they do has a negative effect ultimately on the economy of the society. It is logical to expect that we as members of the society should be very concerned about proper functioning of the society of mankind on earth and to claim that it is seriously important for us to pay attention to how we are affecting the quality of life on this planet. It is up to us to differentiate between the people who are trying to serve the society and the ones who are selfish in taking advantage of others for their own benefit. We should try to distinguish between businesses which are truly helping to improve the society's life and the ones that can be considered useless or by chance harmful.

Then it is again up to us, by way of doing good for the society, that we try very hard to be wise and brave.

- To be wise and understanding, so that we may better recognize the character of the individuals and the truth about the quality of their performance without our being deceived by enchanting words of those who advertise their harmful service or inappropriate product or being ignorant of the better work of some others who may be less vocal.

- To be brave, so that we can perform more appropriately in supporting useful businesses and the better people who are trying to do right and that we may respect the individuals who deserve it.

- To be brave, so that we do not offer, out of weakness, our admiration to those selfish individuals who are only interested in piling up as much wealth as they can and controlling as much power as possible for their domination over the society, nor do we give support out of our temporary amusement or fascination to the products of potentially harmful businesses or to the persons who are doing what is considered useless or expected to be detrimental to our society's future.

This we ought to do by way of promoting the future well-being of the society, so that individuals may be encouraged to pay more attention to the quality of real service they offer, rather than only being money-conscious, realizing that they would not be receiving extra respect or protection because of mere wealth or fame, but to the contrary, they could be facing the society's unfavorable reaction and disrespect for wealth that would surpass the quantity and quality of service performed. Through this approach, we may be able to apply adequate force towards general improvement of the living conditions of the average people and towards getting rid of the very wide financial gaps that exist in the different nations of our world. They exist possibly with some of the very rich having earned much wealth through manipulative ways in money making without the application of their talents in offering useful service to the society while many of the individuals who live in poverty having spent much of their lives in serving their community with honesty.

33

Corruptive Influence of Wealth and Power

There probably exists a variety of intentions among the people who try, in different nations, to be appointed to authoritative positions, some of whom may exert much effort in the struggle towards being elected or selected. Some of these individuals are very honestly concerned about the quality of life in their community, and they are prepared to tolerate self-sacrifices in the way of serving the society well. A few have as their main intention the possibility of abuse of authority for gaining excessive wealth and assurance for increase of power. Others try to take advantage of the available privileges for satisfying other personal interests and to supply the means that would please a few who are favored by them or who may, in return, offer valuable favors later on. Some others try to help their friends join them in gaining combined control of power towards further escalation of their own group's authority.

There may also be some individuals who dishonestly take advantage of people's trust while having access, with authority, to private money or to funds belonging to different levels of government or other organizations. Then, as a consequence of the bribes or other abuse and wasting of large sums, for the sake of a few who possibly conspire to get wealthier or have temporary fun, masses of people suffer from financial and a variety of other problems, whether tolerating the difficulty of driving on bad roads in need of frequent repairs or having to struggle with other malfunctions of the system. Life becomes more difficult for many, ultimately causing undue injury to the economy of the society as the price for the satisfaction or temporary pleasure of a few who are not trustworthy.

Some individuals, in the interest of making as much money as possible, sell at high price what they have bought very cheaply, or at the time their service is needed they charge their clientele very high and unfair costs. Then, in turn, these people may be treated in the same way by some individuals of their own kind when in need of others in the society. Many of us in some communities may present this selfish attitude. Instead, we ought to try to run our business with fairness to others, without being extra eager for having excessive income. Perhaps we could feel content with earning just the adequate amount that we need for our comfort if we lived in an ideal society with the feeling of mutual support and security.

While some of the individuals or groups in business try to make more profit by increasing their prices, there continues to be accelerating inflation, making life more difficult for a very large portion of the population in our society, who are in constant struggle to make ends meet and to survive in the selfish, money–conscious surrounding. For the sake of proper functioning of our society, and as a result, our own contentment, we should try to remember that the priorities in relation to our work and daily activities need to be placed correctly. Our intentions ought to be in the direction of offering the right service to the society, sustaining adequate necessities of life for ourselves and our dependents and enjoying what we do. But we should be very careful not to place these priorities in the reverse order.

Some of the wealthy individuals, just because they can afford it, spend a lot of money unnecessarily in doing what could be achieved very reasonably. At times there is excessive waste of large sums of money because they are spent from the pocket of the business or from another fund rather than by the one who authorizes the expenditure, inconsiderate of the fact that any waste ultimately affects the society's pocket and gross economy in a negative way. The useless extravagance in the life of some people is often not a source of high level of comfort or pleasure, once they become accustomed to it. At times it may even cause related difficulties and problems for them while it can make many families and members of the society miss or lose, in compensation, much of their basic necessities.

Those who spend extraordinarily large sums of money for what they could achieve very reasonably, without much difference in result, such as in travel, the way their food is being served, their place of residence, their transportation, or some unnecessary luxuries, are just ignorant of their act of wastefulness. They behave like little children anxious to buy something, paying a higher price at the store or from a coin machine rather than getting the same kind of item which is available much more reasonably in their homes. Some people who can afford to, waste more and more in totally useless ways, just keeping the money out of the hands of those who need it.

Much is spent by some of our people on a variety of clothes and other means in order to look nicer and more attractive, far above what would be the needed basic supply of clean and proper attire for adequate function in the society. There are very large budgets spent for celebrations and ceremonies that can cause, directly or indirectly, a negative effect on society's economy. Some of these could be arranged much more reasonably, and some perhaps are not needed at all. Some of these activities may even be a source of ultimate loss to the section of the society that supports them because their cause is not noble.

At many celebrations large quantities of food are being served to those who can afford to eat excessively on their own, or sweets and cookies are offered to the people who have problem with being overweight, and presents are exchanged out of obligation rather than affection or necessity. There may be others witnessing the process who have the need but not the means for doing the same, so they may suffer sadness and depression. Perhaps it would help the society more favorably if we adopt the habit of continuing to give as we can afford, fairly regularly, to those who need and deserve, rather than collecting and waiting for special occasions then giving, with a feeling of obligation, to those who have no need.

We should also make those who are in control of much wealth and power realize that we as the members of the society do not give them our support and honor merely because of their being rich and famous, nor out of our being impressed with their unnecessary luxurious wasting or extravagant celebrations. In fact we should insist on making them comprehend the fact that their excessive attraction towards worldly luxuries and extravagant living is neither helping society in general nor does it guarantee the persistence of their own happiness. They ought to understand that the degree of their ongoing pleasure in life cannot be according to the quantity of wealth they have in their control nor the extent of luxury in their living. This is because whenever they become used to what they have above their basic comfortable needs, it all becomes routine for them, and they continue to have a see-saw feeling, depending on other aspects of life, like anyone else would.

They should also appreciate the very important fact that if they enjoy only the material pleasures, when they lose them, they become sad. If most of their satisfaction in life is from their wealth and related matters or due to their position of power or even their family or their physical capabilities, whenever they lose any of these material privileges, they may face difficult times with severe sadness.

On the other hand, if they are less attached to the material luxuries of this world but are pleased with their efforts towards doing good and getting joy out of their intention for doing what is right for all, then when they face material loss or even physical problem and disease, they can have continuation of the deep joy and satisfaction out of their intention of trying to be unselfish in doing what good they can perform for others and what service they may offer to the whole society.

A serious basic problem that we have all over the world, which has a very strong adverse effect on the economy, happiness, and other aspects of our society's life, is the fact that out of the small minority who are in control of most of the wealth and positions of power, those who present arrogance to others and lack proper human qualities, those who act selfishly by taking advantage of what is in their control for their own pleasure while harming the society, and those who use their power to oppress as many people as they can, are still offered a variety of privileges by the society.

These few continue to hurt the masses of innocent individuals or larger groups and nations, as the case may be, through their actions although they know it is the collective force of the very same majority of oppressed hard working people that supplies them with the authority and power that they possess and use against them. Many of the oppressed majorities, on the other hand, continue willingly to support those devious influential individuals or groups because of being amazed by their luxuries, being impressed by the extravagance in their life, or being simply awed by their power, offering them support with much respect and honor, ignorant of the ultimate effect of their actions on the society's future.

Instead, the more decent members of the society should realize that if they adhere to their responsibilities of supporting better people, who are, even in the position of power, living honest and preferably simple lives, void of extravagance and wasteful luxuries, and present their disapproval or criticism to the wrongdoers, then they are taking part in the effort towards correcting the society's problems. If on the contrary, with the feeling of being amused under the influence of emotions and desires, with the sensation of apathy or carelessness about everybody's future, or with the lack of hope in having the unity with or receiving cooperation from other members of the society, they support and respect the wrongdoers for their wealth or position, then they are taking their inappropriate share of adding units of energy for the harmful actions being taken and some portion of encouragement, no matter how large or small, allowing devious and selfish individuals to continue on their wrong path of hurting the society for their own personal gains.

34

Cooperative Efforts to Help or Hurt the Economy

We human beings have a strong tendency towards finding whatever possible excuse we can, so that we may divide ourselves into groups. Formation of many of these large and small groups is beneficial and may be considered as an essential pillar of stability for the foundation of our society and its proper function. There are a variety of groups organized with good intentions, for better achievement of responsibilities, for stimulation of more cooperation, for easier division of duties, for higher success in performance, for more specialized education and the adequate use of talents of individuals with different capabilities, for carrying out difficult tasks, and for many other reasons, including the arrangement of proper competitions between groups to encourage teamwork together with learning of how to use the maximum effort for better performance. With the passage of time on one hand, some different groups join together or may offer their assistance to one another for having better success in advancing towards their common goals. On the other hand, the attitude of opposition, dislike, or at times aggression may be observed between some groups or even among different clusters of individuals of the same group, resulting in many groups and subgroups hurting each other's functions, often unwisely due to inappropriate persuasions by a few individuals or a minority of people in the group who may possess deviously radical or self-serving views.

It has been proven during the life of human beings on this planet that much can be achieved through joining of individuals and groups together in a spirit of cooperation. It is sad that on many occasions even the group which has been formed with benevolent intentions can change the direction of its function under some misguided influence. At the same time some groups may be organized with a devious design from the start. As the functions of the groups are very different, some being in accord or harmony with our total well-being and some antagonizing the society's healthy progress, so can the interrelationships between the groups vary a great deal, too. A very serious underlying cause for the problems between the groups, large or small, is that the judgments and feelings of the majority of nicer individuals of a group can often be turned against another mass of wonderful people of a different group by a few who have devious intentions or ideas but possess strong influence over a large number of the individuals of their group. This issue of developing bias by the members of a group in favor of their own group and, at the time of disagreement with some function of another group, presenting an attitude of dislike by stereotyping the whole body of that group, causes a very high degree of ongoing damage to our society and its economy.

The behavior of some people with **prejudice** in favor of their own group and against others can be observed in a variety of occasions in the society's daily activities. When some clients are mistreated by a person at an office, a firm, or some organization, if they complain to that person's supervisors, often the supervisors, with apparent feeling that there should exist a mutual support in the group, protect their own employee against the clientele without attempting to be completely unbiased. When somebody from a group has done by mistake or with malice something wrong to another group or individual, even when the wrongdoing has been disclosed to the public, often the peers of the one who has done wrong, whether family members, friends, or colleagues and supervisors at work, try to make excuses for that person or cover up the fault, instead of trying to be equally fair to both sides.

I believe these behaviors of prejudice with unfair partiality exist in an appreciable number of people at different levels of our society all over the world. Not all of the individuals in a particular group have the same level of moral qualities or human values, nor do the members of the group have equal authority or influence on the function of the group. No matter what basis the group has been formed on, there usually are a few members who have more power of control over the function of the majority. There can also be in any given group a few who are having more influence on the final action of the group although those few may not necessarily be the ones who have apparent authority.

The actions of those with authority do not always reflect the true intentions of the whole group or the majority. We are suffering a great deal of loss in every nation of our world through the inappropriate manipulation of the feelings and actions of large or small groups against one another. On each occasion the few in a group who have more influence and/or authority may, with malice or by mistake, turn the views of the majority of the individuals of their own group against some others or, through their dominance, force their people to hurt the other group. With this act of sabotage they disrupt or prevent useful cooperation that could exist between the two groups, replacing it with acts of injury of different types. As a result they abolish the positive points which could have existed towards the betterment of the society, replacing them with some damage to the function and ultimately creating negative points for the general well-being or the economy.

Yet their efforts which are detrimental to the society may not have a lasting benefit for their own group either. These individuals may use the influence of their words and authority to successfully enrage their own people against the other group with false representation, which may result in escalation of hate between them and continuation of unnecessary hardships and stressful lives for many people in both groups, so that what they want is done to secure their own positions or advantages or to satisfy their selfish desires, ignorant that problems can continue to be the outcome, hurting both groups, making life more difficult even for their own people.

Many a time the malicious or **corrupt leaders** and influential members of a group, in the garb of trusted friends, can harm their own people much more effectively while performing from within the group than the known enemies could do from outside. Some vicious influentials by way of securing control over the groups may intentionally keep them in constant disagreement and quarrel with one another. When an action that we consider wrong is taken by a group, we can neither blame all of the members of the group equally for what has been done, nor criticize everybody who is among the few with authority since they may not all be sharing the fault but only some of them bearing the guilt with awareness of the detrimental results of their persuasions.

Those with authority in a group do not all have equal levels of honesty and benevolence. The larger the group, the more diversity we may find among the characters of those in control of the group's actions. When in a position of power, they may present a wide variety of attitudes towards people of their own group and others. Some of these individuals, even if selected or elected by the body of the group, may become so engaged with the luxury and privileges at their disposal that they show arrogance to the members of their own group. No matter how little or great a power they may possess, they show off in the presence of others, and when dealing with the average of the same people who have given them the authority, they may oppress them in different ways to the extent of their abilities.

They may do much that is to their own advantage but to the disadvantage of the majority of people, and although originally they were among and part of the same majority, after being in their position of power for awhile, they gradually behave as superior to and separate from the average individuals of their own group. To do this more successfully, they may join some others, who have positions of influence and similar personal qualities to form a powerful selfish lobby or team, forcing the majority of their people to obey them at will or per obligation.

The degree of their **capability to manipulate** their group into believing what is incorrect and doing what is wrong varies, depending on many factors. The most important among these factors perhaps would be the level reached by the average members of the group in **education, faith, discipline, moral values, and human qualities**. It is very important for the mass of the majority to have been nurtured well with different aspects of education and to develop the ability of adequately differentiating between right and wrong and of properly controlling their emotions, so that their thoughts and actions cannot be easily manipulated towards believing what is wrong and doing what is inappropriate. Proper education may be a successful solution to the problems existing between the groups of our society.

When the majority in a group insists on having right views, correct words, and appropriate actions, they may succeed with their firm and proper approach to bring about needed improvements for the whole group. For having orderly function, the members ought to follow the instructions given by those among them who have the authority over the group, but with their strong expectation of keeping the group's function void of faults and vices they may create an atmosphere of goodwill. The whole group can then show its disapproval of wrongdoing so firmly that the wicked individuals either do not get to be in the positions of much power and influence, or they will be compelled to incarcerate the vicious part of their personality and to keep their acts clean. Through this dedicated, cooperative approach, the majorities with the right education and strong human qualities can perhaps neutralize the wrong influence of the very small minorities who may behave as the masters, trying to implement, through the abundance of their wealth and power, more and more control over the hardworking masses of the majorities.

The **benevolent** majorities of different groups may then cooperate together and try to help one another, no matter what size their groups are, whether as small as only a few people or as large as a whole nation, a country, a religious sect, a race, or the representatives of a profession, whose cooperation, with mutual confidence and trust, can in turn help them in advancing towards their common goal of making our surroundings healthier and life much happier on earth. The individual members of such a group could try to keep their thoughts and feelings void of prejudice, realizing that even at times of unfriendly interaction between authoritative persons of their group and those of another group or some conflict of interests between them, they should avoid stereotyping.

They recognize the fact that it is not right to have a similar attitude of approval towards all of the members of one group or dislike for everybody in another group since we all cannot be certain what attitude we would have if we were, due to a variety of circumstances, in a group completely different from what we are. While we may, for proper function of the society, belong to different groups, it is very logical and wise if the better people of the different groups try to have friendly inter-relationships in assisting each other and promoting the improvement of life and economy of the whole society and the health of this magnificent planet.

If the members of any group feel a threat to their proper function due to the wrongdoings of their leaders and authoritative persons, as long as the individual members possess the better human qualities, they can show their disapproval so firmly that they may cause the necessary correction of the actions or ultimately the change of the authorities when so required. If instead the people in the group fail to strive towards perfection of the quality of performance of their individuals, and when displeased with the actions of their leaders they submit to aggressive and possibly violent or rebellious acts to replace them, they would face two problems:

1. The imminent problem is that in the process of revolting against their leaders, probably following the encouragements by some in the group who are taking radical and by chance extreme approaches, they cannot guarantee that those who are the replacements, per choice of those radicals, are going to be better individuals, definitely not any worse than their existing leadership.

2. The second problem is that if most of the individuals fail to improve their personal qualities to the extent needed for deserving the right leadership, if they surrender to their emotions following devious persuasions of others, and if they do not, as a group, adhere strongly to their principles of presenting the proper attitude and having the right expectations, there can be reassurance that no matter who gets to be in charge, the corruptions will find their way to affect their group again.

If we people, who constitute the groups, are good, do what is proper, and expect what is right, we may succeed in severely hampering the manipulative power that some radicals with selfish intentions try to exercise over our groups. Then, our majorities can, with benevolence, show adequate collective courage in doing right. They would promote good deeds and keep from being misguided to do wrong, or from approving corruptions of one type or another, or from supporting the wrongdoers even if they possess much wealth and power. This can have unimaginable effects on improvement of life and correction of economic problems of our society.

If the mass of people of the society do not try to have adequate levels of education and intellect needed for keeping them from being easily deceived into believing what is incorrect or manipulated to do what is wrong, and if they do not reach the point of having proper mutual cooperation between better people of our nations as a powerful understanding unit, the future of human race and the freedom of our coming generations in their lifetime can be seriously endangered through more and stricter control practiced over the groups.

If very small minorities who are eager to earn as much wealth and power as possible, while having selfish and dishonest intentions, manage to be in control over the great majorities of our people in this world, they may be successful, in the presence of the rapid advancement of technology, in learning more and more centralized information about the masses of the people of the nations and countries and in gaining the means of applying tight manipulative control over them. They may find legal excuses or illegal techniques of invading the population's privacy to gather information about everybody. They may collect data about people's daily schedules, habits, telephone conversations, and other private correspondence or communications about social life, defaults, health status, professional or habitual strengths or weaknesses, and other particulars in life. Then, even at the time that these authoritative figures conspire to apply the most serious of injustices towards their own nation, anybody who contemplates to initiate some action towards criticizing them or weakening their position of control can be, through very legal approaches or other means, dealt with aggressively and the activities against their authority nullified, so that nobody from the honest majority would dare or could try to oppose their power.

This might happen in any country, no matter what kind of democratic or other system of government is in force. Ideally, in any group there should be a strong spirit of bilateral confidence and cooperation between the body of the intellectual members and their trustworthy leadership. For example, in regard to any particular country, at the same time that the members of the government should be efficient and honest, for correction of the problems they need the assistance of the masses of the people. The governments may be able to enforce some rules or laws temporarily, but finally it is up to the people of the country to make what is enforced practical. In fact, in the long run, what the people really want is going to be what the governments will have to carry out. If the majority of the people seriously desires to cooperate with those in authority, towards correcting the problems of their country and the whole society, this may better guarantee sustained improvements. The leaders will ultimately have to follow the way that the mass of intellectual, serious, understanding and reasonable people, while united together, is pursuing aggressively. So, the correction of the problems related to our economy should be truly started at our level, i.e., the members of the society.

35

The Game of Playing with the Rules

Part of the problems of economy at the present time in our society stems from the actions of some lawyers, in the same way that some engineers, some physicians, some politicians, and some of the members of other professions and businesses can be blamed for these problems. If some of the students of a profession have as their main goal upon entering their career the opportunity of great financial success, without real concern about offering to the society adequate valuable service in exchange, they may become the source of much injury to the society's well-being and economy. This fact can be true in reference to any profession, more or less in the same way that applies to the study and practice of law. Although good lawyers who exist in different countries and communities are necessary for many aspects of the society's function, we cannot expect all of the lawyers to be good since, like any other large group of people, the lawyers have a wide range of human qualities. While many lawyers may promote virtues and valuable improvements in our society, some may cause hardship for people and ultimately damage our society's economy. Since, in this book, I am looking critically at the defaults of our society, I am not planning to elaborate much in these paragraphs on what good is done by most of the lawyers, but I would like to refer to what is possibly done by some that can be detrimental to the society's contentment and comfort.

It is wrong if some lawyers insist on encouraging the people that, instead of forgiving, they should file claims against one another in an effort to receive compensation for damages when there has been injury which is truly not due to anybody's fault. Perhaps our society is suffering from enormous physical, emotional, and financial stress as a result of court proceedings and other activities related to many such claims, causing the waste of society's time and other resources in order that some individuals may earn a luxurious living easily, instead of spending their time in a productive work or some function that can support the productivity of others. As it is true for many other professions, we can claim that some lawyers reinforce the productivity of others, and some lawyers can cause damage, while taking undue advantage of the productive mass of society. It is wrong if some lawyers defend the criminal as innocent, with knowledge about that person's guilt, and if they try to save the guilty individual from receiving appropriate punishment. This would be using the professional obligation as an excuse while spending their time in fighting the innocents and helping the one who hurts the society.

Whether they do this by way of earning recognition, fame or finances, in any case this can be considered selfish effort for personal interest at the price of ultimate damage to the society's comfort and economy. It would be sad if with their help the punishment, which is supposed to be an evident deterring lesson to wrongdoers and other potential future criminals, is relinquished, when that criminal returns to the society with the tendency of committing more vicious crimes, this time having less fear of the society's justice. It is also sad if some criminals who deserve severe and swift physical punishment, or the murderers who should be executed, are placed in long term confinement, having all of their basic or above basic necessities like food, shelter, medical, and other care supplied and paid for by the society, not even having the obligations towards supporting the society while at the same time there may be innocents in the same community who are homeless and hungry, searching for protection from the frost of winter or heat of summer.

This I consider wasting of the talents, education, and expertise of some lawyers, when used in the way of hurting, rather than helping or favoring, the productive innocent sector of the society. How nice it could be if the lawyers and others, after becoming aware of the criminal's guilt, would help rather than fight the system of justice to apply the proper severe punishment to the point that the individual members of any community would know that a criminal is prone to receive quick and severe punishment appropriate for the committed crime and will have difficulty in finding anyone to help towards covering up the guilt. This would be the proper use of the time and intellect of the lawyers in the direction of supporting the society and its productivity. It is wrong if in some communities the system of justice and the practice of law are manipulated to the degree of corruption that the final outcome or result in the legal confrontations does not depend mainly on who is right or wrong and the innocence or guilt, but on which side has more influential legal support. And if in some communities one who can afford to pay very high legal fees may simply get by committing almost any crime without receiving the deserving punishment.

It is wrong if some lawyers, in the process of filing claims on behalf of their client against someone else, in the interest of having more income for themselves, try to aim for compensations far above what would be fair. They may succeed in receiving excessive sums of money with the excuse that it is paid by the insurance company or other source that could afford the payment. It should be remembered, though, that they are after all paid from the society's pocket, and if their earning is more than what they deserve, they are generating negative points for the general economy. And, when people are encouraged to keep on filing claims against one another for whatever excuse they may find, the members of the same community will have to pay higher and higher insurance premiums.

Perhaps one problem is that on many occasions the lawyers have their income depending on the volume of claims filed and the sums of awards and settlements received. This could be an incentive for some, making them eager to aim for excessively high demands. It is wrong if some lawyers use their influence in the systems that govern our society's functions, such as the different levels of government, the law enforcement, the judiciary system, the financial institutions or the legislative force, in order to dominate small and large communities, then try to use their connections to oppress the majorities. By chance they may organize groups with invisible connections in support of one another that can manipulate important functions of the communities and society to the point that the innocent majorities in a small town or a larger section of our society would not dare nor feel capable of opposing them properly, even in the case of their wrongdoing or serious abuse of their power.

It is wrong if as a result of the possibility of some lawyers having had extraordinary success in establishing extravagant lifestyles with very high incomes, that some of them may deserve and some do not, many of the talented young ones proceed to study law, with the intention and hope of having very high achievements, to the point that there would be graduates of law in abundance, far above the number needed for a healthy community which is trying to have the fewest mishaps, defaults, and crimes. This could generate two problems for the community in consideration.

One important loss can be the wasting of the bright minds and the costly education of some individuals who have studied well but do not find decent work that would be suitable for their status. The other problem is the possibility that out of the large number of lawyers available in excess of their community's need some, who do not have very high human qualities for somehow making a living close to the level of luxury that they expect, may get involved in actions to secure their influence and income without adequate useful work for the society. Some may get involved with minor or major wrongdoings. Some may try to be in influential positions of the community and then manipulate the rules and laws to their own advantage and to the desire of the ones who are favored by them. Some may use their knowledge and qualification to find legal excuses and loopholes in supporting, against innocent majorities, others who are hurting the society in a variety of ways through their wrong activities or the harmful businesses they run.

Others might possibly condone for their community the lifestyle that can generate more possibility for their involvement with legal confrontations so that they can secure the people's ongoing need for their service with reassurance for sufficient continuous income, inconsiderate of the resultant damage caused to the society, to its productivity, and to the economy for all. Some may promote, through their influence, many difficulties for their community, so that their own involvement or assistance becomes indispensable in almost every simple or complicated procedure related to the routine activities during the normal life of the society and as a result of magnification of the problems. This may make their help needed, even for reading and understanding a contract or paper related to an ordinary transaction, to interpret the difficult language of their colleagues and for preparation of an equally difficult to understand correspondence or reply.

This can become a vicious cycle if they manipulate, through the laws and rules, the society's function to the point that for any simple procedure the execution of contracts or preparation of the difficult legal papers becomes a necessity, per insurance requirement or other reasons. The need for the service of their honest colleagues is very true. Even at a time that somebody becomes the victim of the wrongdoing of a lawyer, to be able to file a complaint, that person would probably need to seek the assistance of others from the same profession. Still, one would feel sorry for possibly many talented lawyers, who may be wasting their valuable time in doing jobs which are too simple for their qualifications while they have difficulty in finding suitable positions and adequate income which they may deserve.

36

To Tackle World's Problems of Economy

The present problems related to the economy of our society in the world are of great importance. The main part of these problems may easily be solved if we, the same people on earth who are both causing them and are hurt by them, cooperate together to correct them. It can be claimed that these problems are basically related to the availability and management of resources. The availability of funds and resources is effected by the ratio of the total production to overall consumption of the needed materials and services. In an attempt to correct our society's financial problems we have to apply our collective efforts towards correcting the three deviated factors, namely: the magnitude of production of quality resources; the proper control of the rate of consumption of the resources, including aggressive reduction of wasting; and the correct management of the use of the supply available to our society as a result of the balance between production and consumption. Leaving any of the three factors to remain crooked may prove our efforts towards correction of the problem to be futile.

The same would be true if in our corrections or calculations we disregard the fact that the whole society of mankind in this world is a unit with the economic problems of its different parts being somehow interrelated with ultimate direct or indirect effect on the world's economy. So the efforts to improve our status should be with sincere concern about the betterment of life and the financial stability for the whole unit in general and not only sections thereof.

In the few preceding chapters, I mentioned some of the elements that can have strong effect on the society's economic status. Each of those elements, and perhaps many more that were not mentioned, may have different degrees of influence on the three factors of production, consumption, and management of the society's funds and resources. We may again compare the economic difficulties of our society to the problems related to food shortage and nutrition of a group of people. Mentioned earlier as a hypothetical example was living in a compound with abuse and wasting of the more than adequate farm, also mishandling of the already insufficient food ingredients. We, the people of this planet, ought to cooperate in making better use of the vast farm of manpower and the abundant possibilities that are available to us, by proper appreciation of their value for our present and future generations, and by paying sincere attention to prevent any waste of these priceless opportunities.

Preparation of adequate **family life** for the children of our society and correction in the variety of factors that influence the formation and function of proper family unit, with provision of sufficient level of the many aspects of education, can have ultimately unimaginable effect on the productivity of the society. With such children, more content with the life void of vices and filled with satisfaction from doing good, becoming better parents for their children, we may have more confidence in the ongoing improvement of the society's happiness, economic status, and quality of life.

We should strongly advocate for **religious, ethical and moral values** in relation to different aspects of life among the young and old generations of our society. This can effectually correct, if practiced right, the whole three elements of production, consumption, and management of the resources. With adherence to some related routines and principles, such as following the proper rules of modesty, chastity and abstinence from promiscuity, many other social problems can be corrected or avoided, and again much more reinforcement of the foundations of family life can be achieved. The respect and concern for these values should be adopted by our younger generation at a very early age, so that the majority of the children of our society grow up strengthening these feelings. Otherwise, later correction may prove to be extremely difficult, and if the mainstream of immorality becomes available, the minority could have a hard time, faced against the evil current while trying to stay in the right direction. In an effort to have proper discipline in the future for our society, our youth ought to learn to be pleased with manifesting decency in their word, in their attire, and in their behavior.

In an attempt to support the family values with stronger bond between two persons of the opposite gender, as the parents of the future generation, with their better success in preparation of the right home environment, society should spend deliberate and continuous effort towards eradicating two destructive but interrelated forces:

- One is the availability in public, of indecent exposure of human body and limbs, whether as pictures which are presented in print or broadcast, as sculptured likeness, or as live appearance by individuals who are careless about the decency of their attire and the importance of trying not to expose themselves in public in a manner that can arouse lustful temptations.
- The other is the practice of unethical romance or promiscuity and the availability of a variety of elements in the society that encourage this behavior, such as provision of the circumstances at work, school, social gatherings, and elsewhere in the society, that promote the wrong temptations; or presentation of immorality and promiscuous relationships by the entertainment and related industries.

These two destructive forces have to be fought aggressively, so that the two potential parents can continue to feel, with mutual confidence, a powerful attraction to, and need for, each other, without the society's bringing to them strong means of devious temptation to weaken their attachment, or to become accustomed to so much unethical freedom and variety that they cannot keep their romantic appeal for one another. With elimination of the two above-mentioned destructive forces, marriages can achieve a much stronger bond since the two persons of the opposite gender may search and find in themselves what they need for complementing each other without comparing their physical and behavioral characteristics to other possibilities and may enjoy longer-lasting attachment since the society would not try to destroy their mutual happiness by persistent presentation of evil forces that can cause distractive temptations. Instead, the society should devise ways to support the joining of youth in marriage and the establishment of prosperous family environment for an adequate number of individuals of the next generation.

The speed of exhaustion of our resources is directly related to our overcrowding of this planet. To encourage proper ways of **family planning**, so that we may have close to the optimum of the quantity and quality of people living on earth, would better guarantee the adequacy of our resources, and proper control of the overall rate of their consumption, so that, by having close to the right crowd on the surface of earth, and by avoiding harmful overpopulation of parts of it, there would be more and more of a satisfactory balance between the production and consumption of needed materials and services. Yet, the abundance of supply of what would be required for the society's comfortable life, or existence of the right balance between the production and consumption of these resources by having an optimum number of people for using them, does not by itself guarantee the society's ongoing economic stability or contentment. The way the available funds and resources are put to use is more important than the adequacy of their quantity.

I have already discussed some of the ways that the management of these resources is influenced by the many aspects of our lifestyle. In fact, just about all of what I am writing in this book can have some kind of direct or indirect relation to this management or the mishandling of the resources of our world. As mentioned earlier and repeated in this book, society should adopt ways of promoting a fair division of available resources among its individuals. This has to be done, for obtaining satisfactory result from the more homogeneous application and usage of the funds and resources, and towards offering better average quality of life for the whole society. The individual members and the society as a whole can encourage the one who affords to donate voluntarily, through showing an attitude of not giving honor and support for mere wealth but to the person who is trying harder to be good and do what is right for the society. They can insist on showing respect for the proper human qualities and disrespect for luxury which is not accompanied by admirable personal qualities.

If we want to proceed towards correcting the economic problems of our society, we as individual members and collectively the society as a strong unit, should take big steps towards correcting our lifestyles. We ought to establish ways that strongly encourage everybody **to be productive** rather than being a successful parasite or a bum, to be honest instead of cheating, to be fair rather than yielding to favoritism, to be faithful rather than dishonest, to be modest rather than indecent, to enjoy a healthy family life rather than be promiscuous, and to be pleased with donating to support the needy rather than being only selfish and miserly.

We should discourage the mechanisms in the society by which the rich find momentum for becoming richer and richer, and the honest poor are left to get in deeper poverty, and the big businesses get bigger by swallowing the smaller ones which become deserted or bankrupt, closing down one after another. We have to provide the mechanisms through which better people feel safer and more content, rather than the parasites who in clever ways take advantage of the efforts of others. Instead of respecting or honoring the rich for mere luxury of what they own without consideration of the quality of their human values, our society should discourage them from trying to collect as much wealth as possible without using it in a socially beneficial way.

Those who are eager to be in control of as much money as they can, far above what they could possibly use for their needs, are like a person who would be collecting and storing water as much as possible, far in excess of what is necessary for drinking, washing and other uses, even if there is a possibility of drowning in that excessive storage of water, while keeping it out of reach of those who do not get enough supply for their genuine thirst and basic needs.

One essential problem that causes many individuals to become exceedingly zealous in collecting and keeping as much money as possible is the lack of feeling of **financial security** in the society, by not trusting that in case of need, such as the time of disability or old age, adequate care according to the condition of each individual would be available. We ought to try to correct the attitude of the members of our society so that each of us, like many who already are, would be more concerned about the financial security of the whole society than the economic status of their own. Another problem is that many of us assign to the rich individuals more and more fame, honor, and support, directly proportional to the amount of wealth, luxury, and social influence that we find in their control, no matter how they have earned their money and power or how they make use of them.

If at the same time that we are trying to save for our personal future security, we also provide support to improve the economic status of the society and reinforce the spirit of co-operation and the feeling of obligation or duty for looking after the ones in legitimate need, then we can please our conscience for having done what is right for all. We can enjoy the benefit of any improvement of the society as we and our dear ones are part of the same, and we may feel better assurance that in case of need, in the same way that we look after others, the others may take better care of us. Yet, we are not to do the good to others just by expectation of future compensation, but fulfilling our social duty.

If it is true that at present about ninety percent of the finances of our society are owned and controlled by some ten percent of the people in the world, it would be interesting to make a deduction that in case those ten percent of the people become suddenly inspired to give away only half of what they control to the other ninety percent of our society, the ninety percent of the people all over the world can become about four hundred and fifty percent wealthier. This by itself could not guarantee a very high degree of sustained improvement in the average quality of life on earth. Even following that kind of imaginary process, if we, the whole society, continue to be on an illogical and selfish trend with the existing mistakes of our lifestyle, the sudden multiplying of the assets of the individuals and families does not mean that most of them are going to spend what they get wisely. If we do not follow the proper social, ethical, and human values, the sudden high magnitude of increase of finances alone may be accompanied by corruption and manifest detrimental individual and social results.

At the same time if, following such a process, we continue to be selfish and **miserly**, then after possibly a short period of time most of the assets of our society would again return to the hands of a small number of people. But if donating is accompanied by good intention, in that the rich give to the ones who need not only money but also unselfish advice and help in trying to improve the life of all society of human beings, and with the wealthy learning to feel the joy from continuous offering with goodwill, financial and other assistance as needed, and if this is done with sincerity, we may all benefit, and the rich and poor continue to feel much more pleasure and satisfaction in life.

While the society is providing for individuals the confidence that in case of genuine need, due to disability or otherwise, they will be adequately supported by others, at the same time they should be seriously discouraged from the abuse of this privilege. In fact, those who are capable to work should appreciate their capabilities and be pleased with their lack of need for such abuse. At the same time that adequate financial and other supports are provided by the society to the ones in need, giving of these supports has to be correctly prioritized so that those who receive the assistance are discouraged from wasting it for misguided or useless spending. The attitude of wasting the society's resources in vain, whether on a small scale by individuals or large quantities by groups, should be prevented. Also the society can support its productivity better by not offering awards and recognition to useless performances, but to the people with achievements that are in accord with promoting a better future for all.

For correction of economic problems of the society the efforts of the governments and the advisors knowledgeable in mathematics, economics, or income tax will not be enough. The correction of the basic problem needs to be done by **us, the individual members of the society**. Once we function well by providing an abundance of what is needed for us, when we have the right crowd and are using the available supply properly, then the ones in charge of calculations and organization may play with the figures and manipulate the related policies so that we perhaps live more comfortably. But first we have to cooperate as members of the society to get rid of our problems as much as possible.

We may not achieve these goals if we are just money-hungry, each of us struggling to find ways for pulling the money out of the hands of others. We must consciously try, as individuals and as groups, to be less selfish and more concerned about the welfare of the whole mass of people and about how we can possibly do our part in helping the whole society live more comfortably and be saved from the present problems of the economy; of course, at the same time we are:

a- concerned about ourselves as individuals and groups,

b- trying to earn and save adequately for future security,

c- concerned about the financial contentment and other needs of those who are close and dear to us, and,

d- cautious in spending according to what we can afford at any given time, rather than having the tendency of spending at the limit that we can, then being more or less continuously in shortage of finances.

This is, as mentioned elsewhere in the book, like a crowd of people needing to exit from a building when the place is catching fire. It requires action, cooperation, and unselfishness. Each individual needs to be concerned about safety of self in getting out, but more concerned about the safety of the whole group by helping others get out and assisting to extinguish the fire. If there are possibly a few persons who are very selfish in rushing to get out even at the expense of pushing others back by way of saving themselves, they may cause panic and disruption of cooperative order, resulting in suffocation and burning of the mass of people including some of the same selfish individuals. We all have to do our part in helping others and our society in general, so that we may put out the fire of problems, economic and other kinds, before this destructive fire spreads more and more, burning and injuring continuously the society, including our dear ones of now and in the future.

Selfish persons, who are hampering rather than helping this cooperative effort of improving our society, are greatly misguided. I mean those who knowingly hurt the society for their own temporary gains or the pleasure of their favored few. While these individuals are hurting the whole mass of present

and coming generations, they have their limited attention at any moment, concentrated on their own financial profits or losses. They may be:
- engaged with production and sale of alcoholic beverages, cigarettes, or other substances of addiction, or
- running the places that promote wrongdoings for the young and old, or
- owning casinos and gambling houses, or
- causing financial and other injuries through their acts of crime of small or large scale, or
- sacrificing the safety and comfort of many in the struggle for assuring the security of their own wealth and power, while disturbing the integrity of the society of mankind through generating and escalating hate and enmity, rather than friendship, among the innocent people of groups and nations, or
- deceiving the productive members of our society all over the world in countless other ways.

They are so overwhelmed by the treasures and material life of this world that they are like the alcoholic in the state of intoxication, their view and mind having become confused and blurred. They do not comprehend the truth, nor can they see the real pleasure. They are struggling to get more and more of what they are addicted to, with their intoxicated mind not even paying attention to how they may hurt others through their actions. These individuals are trapped in a vicious cycle that may not interrupt its function until it is too late for them to get the opportunity of enjoying the true feeling of being one member of the whole society with deep satisfaction, from each individual's concern for the whole mass and from the sharing of pleasure with others. These persons should try to clear their minds and open their eyes properly to see the real world around them when they do not have the luxury of materials to block their view from appreciation of nonmaterial joy.

If we correct the multitude of problems that exists with direct and indirect effect on the economy of the society in different parts of the world, such as the few that I referred to in the preceding pages, we may get to the point of sensing such an enrichment by having in the society's possession an abundance of the necessities for a wonderful life, that we will neither have to worry about, nor find the need for extra financial resources. This can happen if we try hard enough to do what is logical for the ongoing well-being of the society; that means if we do the following:

- Pay proper attention and do what can correct and improve the variety of elements that have an effect on the balance between the production and consumption of materials and services needed for a comfortable life in our society and the proper management of this supply,

- favor those individuals and groups who are truly using their efforts towards helping the society and its future, rather than giving our support out of satisfaction of personal desires or emotions to the wrongdoers, as some individuals do. For example, people who, in spite of knowing that pornography increases indecency and crime, still purchase the related publications and watch the movies and other productions of pornographers, or people who give their vote of confidence and financial support to individuals of ill-repute from politicians, athletes, entertainers, religious speakers, or other professionals, due to emotional attachment or out of fascination with their speeches and lies,

- try to support the spirit of cooperation and the attitude of friendship among the better people of different groups from all over the world, promoting peaceful interactions for mutual advancement towards a better life without hurting each other as groups or individuals,

- cease honoring individuals for wealth or fame and show them clearly that the abundance of wealth without exercise of adequate good deeds and admirable human values can be the cause of disrespect and criticism,

- courageously try to get rid of the variety of corruptions related to moral, ethical, and sexual behavior in the society and correct other defaults of our lifestyles, and

- show determination among our decent majorities in different communities and sections of the society in standing united and firm against the few selfish but influential persons among the leaders of groups or those with positions of authority who, in the interest of their own desires or to safeguard their position of power, place parts of the society against other masses of nice people, following their own selfish or radical views, insisting on the attitude of revenge, retaliation and show of force, using negative and harmful propaganda in advocating hate rather than friendship among the people of our world, making life more risky and difficult for masses of innocents, and often carelessly for their own people, too.

If we live such a life, the problems of economy can be overcorrected, perhaps to the point that we will have resources in excess of what we need for keeping us generally comfortable at our present pace of operation in the society. We may then be able to reduce the hours and days of work for the average individual, while having income in excess of need, with abundance of the necessities at a lower price for all. I am confident that if the people of this great society on earth cooperate towards putting their efforts together seriously to correct our major problems, then with our people producing a lot while caring not to waste much, we may get to the point of having most of the basic needs, or what would be the essentials for everybody's sustenance, at our disposal almost for free.

In such a society, made of people who try to give more than there would be need for, there could be such an excess of available funds for helping those in need and such a reduction in the number of the needy not already cared for, that nobody would feel the need to struggle with hardship just for the sake of making more money, but all would be working as hard as they please, enjoying what they do at whatever level, with the feeling of mutual support and concern that would exist between the individuals and the society. Then, the mass of people would have time to spend in doing a lot with their family and community, they would have the resources to use in helping their close ones, and they would have a clear mind and conscience to let them see the real beauties of this world and enjoy the true nonmaterial pleasures in this life.

37

The Need for Unity

People have the tendency of separating themselves from each other as large or small groups. Psychologists call this clannish behavior. This has been evident throughout the history of the life of mankind on this planet. It takes deliberate effort to keep these groups in mutual cooperation and friendship, encouraging them to help each other in the maintenance of a world of beauty and harmony, preserving the life filled with real pleasure and comfort for all. Instead, the groups have often proven not to present sincere help and assistance to each other. At times they hurt or harm each other, either because of being selfish, or due to conflict of interests, or due to senseless frictions and clashes in the past.

One of the strongest means of our separation has been religion, when contrarily this powerful force should work to create a strong bond to keep us together.

This most effective tool has been used by the benevolent to encourage wonderful people of all generations to hold each other's hand, helping those in need, promoting goodwill, making life more pleasant and comfortable for their fellow man, increasing the flow of trust and confidence in their hearts, supporting the better persons towards gaining valuable achievements, and at the same time trying to cleanse their souls and lives from evil intentions, behaviors and actions.

Those among us who, by way of seeking power, are looking for the means to attract the support of a group of people, find religious attachments to be a most suitable tool to keep their followers bonded together but in their control. Some leaders make use of this support, offered unselfishly by groups, in a proper way towards serving the society while some others abuse it.

Small and large groups are formed in the name of religion, and they may divide into smaller groups and sub-groups. At times hatred or clashes may be observed even among those who supposedly belong to the same religious affiliation.

We people have the tendency of narrowing the visual field of our mind, at times seeing with clarity only what we like to see or what we believe in, excluding from our view any other possible scene. Following repetitive suggestions, after we are convinced in believing something, we may gradually develop strong faith towards what is by then, in our understanding, true and considered a fact. We may gradually develop such a bias towards our beliefs that we become blind to any other picture and deaf to hearing an alternative possibility. Those who control the groups benefit from and make use of this quality of ours, insisting upon the truth of what they say, repeating it over and over again. They play with our emotions while manipulating our uncertainties, fears, and affections. They want to keep their power, continuing to receive financial and other support from their small or large group. This is true in most of the aspects of our society's life and not only in relation to religion. This sincerity and faithfulness of the groups are applied by some as a tool in their service to the society, but used by some others to satisfy their selfish goals.

Truly, with proper religious practice we should be able to help one another in saving mankind from most of its problems, but somehow we are not using the right tool in the correct way.

What is religion and how many religions do exist?

Countless groups of people from less civilized cultures and tribes have been observed worshipping a variety of objects considered by them in some way to be superior. Whatever they consider worthy of being worshipped, whether large in size, such as a statue, a tree or a mountain, or having special qualities, such as an animal, or being a source of high energy, such as fire or the sun, or being impressive in other ways, is respected and honored by them to the point that they attach to it supernatural powers. Each group remains separate from others, in that it believes seriously and sincerely only in its own idols. It disregards the idols of other groups and their imaginary powers. Among them can be found persons who may accept belief in A Higher Force, when they are presented logically with the fact that A More Superior Authority has power and control over all of their idols. These individuals, in turn, may help their groups gradually realize the unimportance of their differences and the lack of wisdom in their having unfriend-liness and dislike between the groups.

There is only one true religion, even if we call our practices not by the same name or if we are praying and worshipping in different ways. We all seek to worship The One Supreme Being. The mere existence of this world should be enough evidence to make us believe in A Creator. Since in our world we notice that everything is built and made by some force at some time, this whole world must have been started by An Authority not from this world and not bound to the rule of having had to be created at a point in our concept of time. Since our comprehension is limited to some of the things that we can discover in our world, no matter how hard we try we cannot understand, during this material life, everything about the origin of this world and the fate of our being here. Still, we are all united in this process as we cannot claim that different groups of us have been created by different forces; so, without expecting to understand all about the creation of this world, we have to try to accept it and, of course, believe in the existence of A Creator.

The beliefs to which we have affiliation are all parts of the same religion. We all believe in God Almighty and follow the instructions given by God through numerous bona fide messengers and prophets.

We all agree that there is an eternal life and a day when we shall be judged for our deeds. We can clearly appreciate that we are not only physical machines. Each of us notices the inner feeling of self, with joy and sadness, satisfaction and sorrow, comfort and anger, not only as emotions in appearance but as perceived real feelings, proving that our minds are not just biochemical computers. More correctly, I should claim that I appreciate the above feelings at least in myself.

We know we are something more than this physical existence. How nice it is if we pay less attention to the temporary and fleeting pleasures of our bodies which are assigned to us for a limited use in this world and store more of the everlasting types of joys for our conscience and soul.

The people of so-called different religious practices ought to put their minor differences aside, remembering and emphasizing the binding similarities and common points, above all the main uniting factor which is our belief in The One Creator. Whether we call The Creator God, Lord or other names in different languages, we are all referring to The Same One, The One with infinite knowledge and limitless power.

To confirm their own security, many of the people of each religious group exaggerate the differences in their positions. This is done with the encouragement they receive from some of the teachers of religion. Some of these individuals, while ordained as interpreters of religious law, in order to reinforce their status, strive to have large numbers of followers belong to their group and declare the superiority of their practice or belief compared to the others by presenting stories and writings as evidence to support their claim.

We should insist on the fact that all religious instructions that we are trying to follow have originated from The Same Source, with emphasis on the unifying truth that all of the ones who brought those instructions and delivered the messages were assigned to their duties by The Same Authority. We ought to have equal respect for all those who delivered these messages, accepting that The Supreme Authority is The Only One Capable of judging or comparing their status.

Instead, we have been forming groups, insisting on superiority of one messenger over the others, giving credit to our own people for following the instructions more correctly, compared to the other groups. Each group may exalt the status of a separate prophet with qualities claimed to be above all of the others. Some mention the name of one prophet very often, respecting the stories and books written about that individual almost as much as they respect the revelations from God. Instead of emphasizing only that the people follow the orders given by God through the messenger, they keep mentioning the person of the prophet, stressing their indirect obedience that, since he was almost perfect in following the instructions, the people should trust some reports about what he did and consider his way of life an example for what they should do.

Similar attitude is observed by some people even towards other persons, such as the close companions and followers of the prophets, or the religious leaders whom they consider as perfect examples of behavior. Some assign to their prophet of choice superlative authority, trying to approximate that person to the level of The Creator, rather than stressing the fact that the prophets were physically human beings just like other people, though they had the honorable assignment of delivering the message received from God to the people. Obviously any supernatural powers demonstrated by them were not their own but assigned to them by The Higher Force. We must worship not the agents who delivered the guidance and showed us the light, but only The Source.

Some of us attribute to God Almighty physical characteristics from our material world. Some, while trying to ascertain a more favorite status, mention family relationship with God. This is wrong, even in the allegorical sense. Since God is The Creator and everything in this world is part of the creation, including the people, if we assign to The Creator physical human shape or we mention family relationship between God and ourselves or between God and the prophets, by trying to bring The Creator closer to and involved with the physiological function of our own world, we are being disrespectful to The Creator. There exists only one God with no other little gods. As we believe God to be The Supreme Being, obviously there can be none except only one, otherwise we would be breaking the foundation of our own belief. Some assign special qualities or superiority to their race or group. Some may emphasize the belief that their people are the only ones going to paradise while all of the others are failing the test of life on earth. It is clearly illogical to expect that some individuals would get recognition and eternal reward just because of their group or racial identity rather than their intention and actions.

Having observed a variety of religious groups, there are wonderful people in different gatherings. While not calling their religions by the same name and while having different ways and habits for their prayers, many of them believe in and truly worship the same Supreme Authority. So many have totally different ways of practicing religion because of group customs and traditions, but deep in their hearts they believe in The One Creator and they do understand that there are many other good believers among different groups while possibly some of the members of their own group could be deficient in true faith. Without prejudice, they accept that true superiority is for the person who sincerely believes in God Almighty and tries harder to obey the instructions received from God. Such an individual, who deserves respect, tries to attain proper behavior towards The Creator in performing the applicable religious practices and duties, towards oneself by trying to maintain the standards of being a better person, and towards others by carrying out the duties and responsibilities for offering appropriate services for the good of the society.

38

Brave and Truthful

While observing the different attitudes of the people of our society and the way they behave towards one another, we may notice a couple of interesting facts.

We may notice that the cowards and the ones with two different faces have the tendency of admiring others in their presence and mentioning their faults mainly behind their backs, but the brave people say what is good about others often when they are not in attendance and criticize them in their presence, rather than saying about them in their absence what they would not mention to their face.

We may notice that the better individuals of our society are tough when dealing with the arrogants and are nice and gentle towards the humble and the poor or feeble, but the persons who are not so good with their characteristics and human qualities are often extra polite and flattering towards the arrogant and whomever seems to have more authority in worldly matters or controls a larger quantity of wealth and luxury of this life, but are harsh and rude in their dealings with those who are not considered to be as privileged as they are in this material world.

39

Universal Goodwill

Considering the subjects discussed in this book and the way I have expressed my personal views in these pages, I expect there can be a variety of diverse reactions towards this writing by some of the readers. As requested at the beginning of the book, I would like to insist again on asking that you the reader to make your judgment on the content of this book only after having read it all. Please pay your kind and impartial attention to my reasoning and logic, without letting the degree of your approval or disapproval of what is in this book, and how much you would apply it to your way of life, be affected by any pre-existing bias, by your expectation of the influence of these writings on fulfilling or hurting your personal gains and desires, or by any favorable or unfavorable views that you possibly develop towards me as the author of the book with the quality of my person and the wide range of good and bad that I may have done. If I am good or bad, it does not affect the quality of what is written in these pages.

If you like the writing, please apply it to what you do, definitely without making any issue of the author such as my personal characteristics and name or photograph and other likeness, as this would be exactly in contrast to my suggestion in this book that we should not exaggerate the importance of the individuals but be attentive and learn from their actions. If, on the other hand, you dislike anything that by chance you may know about me, my look, my behavior, or the many inappropriate actions that I may have committed, as I am an ordinary person perhaps with some good and much bad, please do not let that feeling affect your attitude towards this book, so that you continue to be fair towards this writing. At the same time, you would not support or encourage the persons who are accustomed to make rumors, in their struggle to waste your time by offering the true or false and useless information about someone who may not even be a good example for his own writing.

I hope this book is read by many, who may find at least part of it useful in helping them improve their way of life and doing better for the society. To let this book help in uniting the different groups of our people, it is important that the readers be open-minded. Otherwise, different groups may accept parts of the writing, with their partiality, and dismiss what their preconceived thoughts do not let them look at with fairness. They may then continue to insist on their ideas which are causing our unfriendly separations, each group being adamant about its own righteousness, wishing ultimate triumph over others, instead of the groups trying to make logical compromises in the way of getting rid of unwise differences of our beliefs and ideas which are widening the troublesome gaps existing between the various groups.

From people of different levels of our society, some individuals, who feel my writings may threaten their empire of dominance over the masses and their ability to oppress them, may aggressively oppose this book and try to stop people from reading it. But the more benevolent of the same groups, whether they are lawyers or physicians, or politicians, or from the publishing industries and news media, or the preachers of different religions, or the wealthy and famous, will take note of my sincerity and agree with the meaning and truth of what I am claiming or suggesting by way of what must be done to correct our seriously corrupted society. The better people from these and other groups of our society may be successful in promoting universally unselfish goodwill while searching for sensible ways that can encourage our groups, whether religious or otherwise, to pay less attention to our unimportant differences, so that we may find a common ground for our uniting together in friendship and cooperation.

40

cAbsolutes and Optionals

Our life in this world is constantly under the influence of a mixture of factors, a combination of what is done to us by our surroundings, what we ourselves are doing to our surroundings, and what we do to each other. We are dealing with a complex of absolutes and optionals. We try to adjust ourselves to live with what absolutes are here or happening out of our control. We attempt to modify some optionals with the choice that we have and our ability to make decisions. Through this process, in order to have greater possibility of success in reaching worthwhile achievements, we need to plan correctly, proceed properly, and try to live right as would be required for keeping in harmony with the conditions of our habitat and the needs of others who live here with us. While we are making use of so much that has been made available to us, we have the duty of performing our part adequately.

We function with wisdom, and we are pleased with our emotions; we perform with logical reasoning while we appreciate with satisfying the fulfillment of our desires; we live with science, we enjoy the arts; we spend effort in doing the work, then we refresh ourselves with entertainments, all under the control of morality with guidance received from religious instructions. It is important that while we follow the right principles in our life, there should be proper harmony between the different aspects of our functions. There needs to be adequate balance between the applications of science and art, or work and entertainment. There should be proper control by wisdom to justify the desires, and by logic to modify the emotions.

We cannot afford, in this complex maze of life, to get lost while amused with the pleasures, forgetting to use the torch of our conscience to help us advance in the right direction. This is true in every step that we take in this world, trying to advance towards our goals, rather than enjoying our march or dance without consideration for our purpose and the proper destination. For example, if we are employing a teacher for a school we cannot only pay attention to the appearance and attire, but the educational qualification and the teaching abilities are of utmost importance. If the faculty of a school and the student body spend all of their time on beautification of the building and the classes or organization of the meetings followed by recreational activities and sports but they do not pay proper attention to the main objective of the function of the school, which is education, their magnificent reports of meetings and their success in maintenance of the parts of the building and the decorations are all useless.

When we are buying carpet, we pay attention to its being comfortable, functional, durable, easy to clean, and suitable for matching the location, rather than just looking at the color and pattern of the carpet. In marriage, one ought to take into consideration the many qualities, when choosing a suitable spouse to share one's life with, rather than just the apparent attractive physical characteristics.

The same kind of example or reasoning applies in general to our life in this world with the variety of achievements and proper functioning of the whole society. We have to look at the different aspects of our society's function, with the people's performance, achievements, and successes through a logical, and when needed critical view, to evaluate better their ultimate benefit or detriment for the future of all, otherwise much that is abused and can hurt the society and the life of this world may sound as a success and appear as a step forward.

If our wisdom and logic with the guiding morals do not adequately influence our actions, each of us individually can lose the prospect for a decent life ahead, and collectively as nations we may see that the great advancement of our civilization with science and related fields can be manipulated with serious adverse effects on the quality of our society's life and future. Then, with the rapid progress of technology, our society may, instead of benefiting from the improvements, become entrapped in the crooked products of the devious functions of the people who make use of their knowledge without the boundaries of proper ethics, causing the whole society to suffer, including those who can be blamed for such actions.

Although the picture of dominance of the mindless machines over the society of understanding people is usually a science fiction story and may be presented in the films for entertainment, if we are careless with unethical use of the computers and related technology, the interrelated system of computers and similar devices which are accessible to many people, some of whom may use their devious influence, can gradually become corrupted to the point that the decent sector of the society is not able to counteract what the wicked individuals have done to it. Then, the whole society may become so badly trapped that nobody can get rid of the disastrous pollution, at the time that the people of our nations and society are not united together in propagation of better human qualities, but the computers would be united together with the growth and spread of what wrong seeds have been planted in them.

Once the unethical use of that powerful device is established, there can be persistent disturbance of the society's comfort, through the actions of the wicked minds that exist at different levels of our society and that may take control of it and abuse it for their own devious purposes. Some may obtain confidential or personal information and make use of it for harming. The wrongdoers among those who have positions of power may control and manipulate the bank accounts and financial transactions, the private correspondence, the performance at work, and other business or personal aspects of life of whomever from the nicer majority of the people opposes their wrong actions or threatens their authority.

Such harmful involvement may become so widespread that it can manifest adverse effects on the education of children, the peace of mind of grown-ups, and many other aspects of family and social life. Countless examples can prove to be true in showing the possibility of our society's becoming entrapped in the moral and other serious pollutions of advanced technology because of the corruptive influence of the unwise among us, due to our deficient application and control of ethical behavior.

The reports about the statistics related to our economy and employment, and discussions in relation to our advancement or achievements in the fields of science and technology, or sport and entertainment, and many other aspects of our social functions, will be futile if we do not proceed in satisfying our true obligations and performing according to our conscience to justify our existence in this life. That can be like the example mentioned earlier about the student body and its faculty who are in a school with wonderful functions and reports of social activities but deficient in proper education.

When we discuss or report our achievements, we ought to pay attention to their real value. When considering a variety of statistics and figures, when observing the different contests or competitions and taking part in celebrations or award-giving ceremonies, when reviewing our industrial or national and other progresses or successes, we must pay attention to the real value of all of these functions according to proper useful parameters and indices for the future well-being of the whole society. We have to follow the right principles and ethics, so that we do the right things in their proper order and with correct balance in relation to each other, for the sake of a better future for others and for ourselves and our dear ones of present and coming generations.

41

Boundaries of Freedom

Freedom is a very valuable privilege. At every stage of life, we are anxious to be free. We want to be free from physical or mental sufferings unless we gain worthwhile advantages in exchange. We try to be free from the obligations that cause any difficulty for us without adequate benefit. We want to be free from a variety of restrictions that can reduce our comfort or limit our capabilities. We struggle during our lives to be free from having to do what is against our desires. But the freedom to be right, for us as individuals or as groups, must have limits and be used with proper guidelines. For everyone, the freedom has to be in line with the expectation of a satisfactory future for that person, and the interaction of the individual and group freedom must be in accord with the long-lasting exercise and pursuit of happiness and comfort for the whole society.

The reasoning or the excuse that we are free to do what we want as long as we do not trouble others has long been abused and is invalid. Every individual is tied with actions and behavior to the other members of the society. If one's indecent outfit or presentation in the society does not hurt anyone instantly, it can be a factor of encouragement to lead the society in adapting to that incorrect attitude. When, in public, a person's behavior or the manner of dress and make-up arouses lustful temptations in young or old, this is an action with a chain of reactions, causing a multitude of problems for our society. If the producer of a program or talk show on television or radio allows a criminal, a sexually perverted individual or a person who runs a business which is clearly causing damage to the society to be presented to the public without adequate criticism or without being deservedly ridiculed, this can be a harmful lesson, teaching the innocent society to become accustomed to these kinds of behaviors. While many of us may find that kind of program or presentation amusing to our taste, its poisonous effect can decay the foundations of the future health of our society.

If the children in a family are allowed by their parents to behave towards their elders in a rude manner, talking to the parents and others with disrespect, this attitude should not be considered acceptable by the society without any objection. Although those parents have the freedom of raising their children according to their choice, if they do not insist on their moral standards or the quality of their manners, there is going to be a direct and indirect effect on the future lifestyle of those youngsters and the society to which they belong. We have obligations towards ourselves and towards others. As we are part of the society, what we do in life can have an effect, sooner or later, on the lives of others. I may consider myself free to decide how to take care of my personal hygiene, but this would be a responsibility that I have towards myself and the society, as I have to take care of my physical and mental well-being, not only to be able to live better and perform right for the society, but also for trying to be a good example for the ones who may be influenced by my actions.

We as young or old are, more or less, affected all the time by what we may call peer pressure. The way we dress, the way we eat, the way we do our work, the way we drive our car, the way we go on vacation, the way we speak to each other, the way we choose an entertainment to go to or a music to listen to, the way we study, the way we treat our elders, and the way we educate our youngsters are all under the influence of how we observe the others and obtain positive and negative impressions from what they do. Since each of us has to live right to guarantee a better future for self and do what may promise more joy and comfort for the whole society, we all ought to pay attention to use our freedom and strive towards perfecting what is truly beneficial for the future of all of us, rather than the temporary elements of carelessness or transient pleasures with later ill-effects on individuals or groups.

Teaching the children, at their very early stages of life, proper manners, honesty, religious lessons, interest in reading and learning, respect for the rights of others, generosity, truthfulness, modesty, cleanliness, kindness, punctuality, courage and other proper human qualities is a must. Parents and educators have the responsibility for placing the right seeds in the fertile minds of the very young children, so that at a later time, when grown up, they, as well as their society, can receive adequate nourishment from such fruits.

Considering the fact that our future is very important, with the comfort of our future generations and the future well-being of our world, we should be concerned about adequate preparation of those who are to do their parts in shaping the future. We have to supply them, at an early age, with the right education that may help them grow up to be capable of performing this delicate task. This education can help them become ladies and gentlemen, decent in manners, with ability for assisting the society, willing to try in an unselfish way to help one another. This education can reinforce their moral standards and their human qualities with their appreciation of the fact that as members of the society they ought to do what not only pleases themselves, but to consider what is right for the pleasure of all, and above all, to obey The Creator Of All Beings.

Although providing the right education for the young ones can be both difficult and in need of much dedication by us, once we make the commitment and proceed to become accustomed to it, we may find much joy in the process, followed by real pleasure when observing the wonderful outcome of our efforts. When these priceless treasures of our society have become used to being good and doing right, they can enjoy their living well. If we fail to give them the correct education at the right time, and if they grow up not straight but with deviations in their character, correcting the wrong habits may prove to be difficult or at times impossible. It seems that at any age there is, for the majority of us, less probability of correction of the seriously wrong habits through the right advice than the adaptation to the wrongdoings under bad influence such as friendship with the ones whose association we should avoid.

Freedom may be used by us as an extra support, giving us the opportunity of spending our efforts towards doing a tremendous volume of good for our society. At the same time many of us may abuse our freedom as an excuse to let us do what we wrongly desire, against the sensible advice of others, and in contrast to what is beneficial for the future of all.

While it is very important that we do have this freedom which can help us not only do a lot of good but also, through the expression of our opinions, be able to help many others cleanse their actions from mistakes, it is at least equally important that we also try not to be indifferent or careless about how the others make use of their freedom in our society. There should be a general expression of dissatisfaction or disapproval by us towards the behaviors which are clearly in contrast to the future well-being of the whole society. We must have ways of showing continuous support, encouraging the ones who are properly trying to serve the society, at the same time discouraging those who take advantage of their freedom in the society, causing deliberate damage with their words and actions.

To be able to fulfill our duty in this regard, we must control our emotions. We need to apply our logical determination on where and how strongly to show our approval or disapproval of the way others influence the society through their appearance, their speech and their actions. Otherwise, if we are totally free to appear, behave, and perform as we wish, without facing any objection or criticism since many of us can adapt to bad habits more easily than the right ones, the society can suffer gradual but serious deterioration.

42

Guidance, and the Guides

I would like to write briefly about my personal belief or feelings towards the prophets and religious books. I believe in the prophets and messengers of God and respect them all equally. I do not honor as prophet everybody who has claimed unusual capabilities such as foretelling future events or feeling some premonitions. I consider the main religious books, which include revelations from God, all as parts or volumes of the same essential reference, while disregarding some controversies that may be due to human influence and alterations.

I believe we ought to pay more attention to the essential guidance in a way to strengthen our faith in God Almighty, learning how to live a prosperous life, truly following the instructions for being a better person for self and others. The orders regarding how we are to live in this world are generally the same in the books, though they are mentioned and repeated in different ways. We should pay less attention to the allegorical parts, especially the less important items that can cause unnecessary or useless debates and disagreements.

Let us all cooperate in following the instructions properly in order to have a decent life for our society, rather than waste our time or by chance hurt each other and the society over some erroneous controversies in our ideas which can be mainly due to our misunderstanding of the facts. Let us help each other with the strength of our faith in God, rather than hurt our fellow mankind over unimportant differences in the name of religion.

It seems reasonable to expect that if all of the people who are religious, believing in God, no matter what group or so called religion they belong to, try to be united together, there will be tremendous mutual benefit as a result of their friendship. In the same way, it is obvious that if these people have group behavior with unreasonable aggression towards each other, the ultimate outcome of their selfish acts will cause a persistent flow of distress for mankind. If they have the attitude of considering other groups as enemies rather than friends, there will continue to exist problems between the groups instead of sincere cooperation. Even at times when they offer their assistance to each other in carrying out any project or in opposing another group, this gesture is only temporary, which later ceases, once their common mission is over. This kind of behavior can let the individuals of any group demonstrate, even when there is no problem with another group, the tendency of forming smaller groups and sub-groups to face the others with distrust.

We may live well and help in preparation of a peaceful life for the future generations of this planet if we perform as follows:

- We all use our faith as a bonding force to keep us together, leaving aside the elements of disparity.
- We do not consider Arab and Jew, black and white, or any other group or race inferior or superior to one another and realize that it is the character of each individual that counts, rather than having negative or positive points for the whole group.
- The Christians and Muslims or any other group does not exaggerate the position of one prophet of God over all of the others.
- Those who insist on mentioning the name of one prophet compared to the others and form an idol or an example of perfection to follow, insist on just following the message, as it is the word of God, and avoid in any way worshipping the messenger.
- Each group of us neither raises the position of our prophet of choice over all of the others nor causes the formation of groups in continuous struggle to prove or gain superiority.
- We have respect for all of the prophets of God, yet pay attention to the fact that they all tried to deliver to us the message received from The Same Supreme Authority, our duty being to follow the message, not the separate messengers selectively.

Then we will finally become one group with the tendency towards recognizing anyone who believes in The One Supreme Being as one of us. The prophets have been truly the kings. They were not controlling only worldly treasures and a piece of earth with its inhabitants, but guiding and managing universal human qualities. They were not assigned to their positions of power through inheritance nor by use of force and the people's choice, but appointed to their duties by The Supreme Authority. Therefore, I believe we can consider them as honorable majesties and should respect them all alike.

43

Where is the Limit?

There are three issues in our life that, particularly in dealing with these three compared to other aspects of our social and daily activities, we ought to exercise adequate self-restraint and to have contentment with our share and be pleased with our proper limits, regarding both quality and quantity of supply of each of them. This, we must do to improve our chances of having a long-lasting health of mind and body. If without self-restraint we struggle to have a limitless supply of any of these three, we may cause a lot of stress for ourselves and for many others. These three are food, wealth, and sexual pleasure. We may enjoy our portion from each of them at any moment with much more appreciation if we respect our appropriate limits.

In regard to **food**, it is a very good practice to have periods of intentional fasting, as in some ways has been prescribed per religious instructions. Through this kind of exercise, we may increase our ability to control our hand and mouth whenever it is not right for us to ingest what is within our reach, or when it is going to be in excessive amounts. When practicing abstinence and becoming successful in this act of self-control in regard to eating, we may also improve our chances on other occasions of self-control, for example in avoiding the use of the harmful, addictive substances. When we avoid overeating and are careful in not wasting any food, we may also improve our concern for the living conditions of others in the world who are hungry and may be in need of what we could easily spare.

In regard to **money and power**, at any time we may enjoy our status much more if we remember that perhaps many others would be extremely happy with what we have. While we have ambition in life for higher goals, this should be mixed with the intention that whenever we strive to gain more authority in this world, and control of wealth in excess of what is required to satisfy our basic needs, we try to be in a position enabling us to offer better service to the society. If, to the contrary, we try in a selfish manner to get our hands on as many of the luxuries of this world as possible, inconsiderate of what favor or harm we cause to others in this process, we can generate a lot of unnecessary stress for ourselves with much suffering in the struggle to advance towards the goal which is moving away, as we do not have a limit to be satisfied with. So we may taste less of contentment and more of stress. At the same time we may cause, depending on our status and the level of our efforts, varying degrees of hardship and misery for a small or large number of the individuals of our society. While we strive to do better in the society, if we are at the same time satisfied with what we have of the power and materials of this world and try to use them correctly, we may enjoy our lives with both of the pleasures, the pleasure of having what we want and the great pleasure of feeling that we use what we possess in a way that satisfies our conscience.

Regarding **sexual pleasures**, adequate self-control should be practiced at the individual level and also, with cooperation of the people, at the level of the communities. If this is done properly, many serious problems of society can be ameliorated or prevented. For each person, the proper self-restraint in this regard, by observance of the religious and ethical rules, may guarantee a much healthier future, with increase of ultimate total value of sexual pleasures in life, since for the one who refrains from inappropriate indulgence in sexual desires, there can be much more enjoyment in the timely and permissible romantic involvement. If to the contrary, one ignores the proper boundaries and tries to take advantage of inappropriate opportunities, then to get enough pleasure from romance that person needs more of the wrong involvements, to the point of becoming trapped in a vicious cycle with increase of wrong sexual practices and inability of being satisfied within permissible limits. This can lead to a variety of social, mental, physical, marital, and other problems, and the individual may even get involved with totally diverted sexual life and may become incapable at an early age of really enjoying the normal or any kind of acts of romance.

People are in need of cooperating to create in their communities an atmosphere which is void of pollution due to sexual wrongdoings, so that it would be easier for individuals to observe the proper limits. If the people, in general, present the tendency of considering their freedom of exposing their bodies or the pictures thereof indecently in the public and condoning the physical intimacy with touching, kissing, and embracing among the strangers of the opposite gender as signs of social advancement and civilization, then they are preparing a polluted surrounding that makes it harder, even for the individuals who have very clean intentions, to express self-control and persist in observing the limits at all time. In that kind of unclean sexual atmosphere, many young ones may ignore the moral and ethical obligation of self-control and get involved in promiscuity, then by becoming used to having a variety of sexual partners and accustomed to disregarding the religious and other boundaries, they continue the unclean and transient relationships without commitment toward formation of a proper family, or if they marry, there is a probability of their continuing the wrong habits with disappointments, unfaithfulness, and separations.

If we pay attention to a very simple calculation in our mind, without allowing our emotions or animal desires to interfere with our acceptance of the facts, we can conclude easily that the availability of romantic involvements and means of sexual stimulation or temptation in public can be the cause for serious deterioration of the community's and our society's future.

To explain in more detail, we know that the education of the children of the present is of utmost importance for having a better generation in the future. Towards this goal, the proper growth and maturation of these children in a pleasant and suitable surrounding are needed. It is also evident that the children will be happier, and their minds would grow generally healthier when in the early years of their lives they have both of the parents concerned and in attendance. The availability of any kind of romantic and sexually stimulating opportunities in public can clearly cause temptations that can lead to promiscuity with improper sexual relationships or romantic involvements that can generate, among the multitude of major social problems, also serious reduction in the probability of formation or continuation of a strong and permanent bond between two persons of opposite sex which is needed for the establishment of a happy and healthy family atmosphere and required for the proper nurturing of the individual members of future generations.

The wide variety of factors in our communities that stimulate people's sexual desires and the individuals who promote the availability of those wrong influences in public are extremely injurious to our society and its future. In trying to save our society from the potential of devastating sexual corruption and its variety of complications, the better people of our communities ought to exercise serious effort, with determination, to limit the practice of sex and romance and the related stimulating means, to the privacy of the spouses and the seclusion of the bedroom and the like, rather than allow any means of romantic stimulation or what can cause lustful temptations to be available in public. People of either gender should behave decently in public and avoid causing any lustful temptation through their appearance or with their verbal or physical gesture. The communities must avoid the presentation to the public of any materials that stimulate sex, such as inappropriate writings, pictures, films, and statues.

There are many people in our society who are using, inappropriately, what can interfere with their productivity at work. As examples, I may refer to the persons who do not restrict themselves from the abuse of three different means of distraction. There are people who drink **alcoholic beverage** even at the time when it can lead to their being intoxicated during working hours. There are individuals who have **romantic temptations and involvements** while at work, which are not only out of order, but also interfere with their efficient performance at work. And, there are, many people who have so much of **food and edible goodies** consumed at the time of performance of their duties that their nibbling is not only a source of overweight and other impairments to health, but also a distraction, affecting their minds almost as an addiction that they turn frequently to wasting their time by not paying proper attention to their responsibilities of work, and as a result, hurt the efficiency of their performance.

To help the members of our society practice adequate **self-restraint** in regard to different aspects of life, the people of each community must try as a group to keep from encouraging socially harmful behavior and habits. Otherwise, if the commu-

nities generally misbehave and let the broadcasting and publishing industries present as entertainment or for sale as
products, much of which are sexual in nature and other beauties
and luxuries, mixed with moral corruptions, this can cause in
the minds of the masses dissatisfaction about their own status
and what they have and may encourage some individuals to
commit wrongful acts in order to access to those levels of corrupted and imaginary pleasures. In the process, though, there
can be unfortunate loss of true happiness which these people
already had and damage to proper well-being that could be
desired for the society. The result is ultimately a considerable
source of depression to the individuals and much stress for the
whole society.

44

The Price We Pay

Our society is suffering great losses because of crime and criminals. There are decent productive people who are killed or disabled as a result of crime. Much property is stolen, wasted, burned, or destroyed through vicious acts. There are vast numbers of potentially productive persons, wasting their time in involvement with wrongdoing, or they are serving their sentences in prison. Exorbitant budgets are spent on facilities, equipment, and individuals involved with the arrest, trial, and punishment of criminals. Such a large asset of the society, which is being lost, could be used in productive ways. There is also a great loss of time, effort, and money through the continuous concern or worry by the society in general to establish means of self-protection or prevention from becoming victim of crimes.

The people who are accustomed to putting on a big show of support for criminals and their rights try to replace the society's reasonable norms by using misplaced sympathy. Those who seriously criticize my suggestion of being aggressive with early severe physical punishment of criminals should control their sentiments and pay attention to the logic of my suggestion of the potential solution to our serious problem. They may refer to severe physical punishment as being cruel, harsh, or uncivilized. This would be playing with words to arouse incorrectly the society's sympathy towards criminals, resulting in dangerous future consequences.

The same people with misplaced sympathy probably agree that when somebody has an organ and part of the body, or even an extremity, affected by gangrene or other serious disease to the point that the concerned physicians feel the medical treatment without urgent surgical operation and removal of that part can seriously endanger the life of that person, the diseased area or extremity should be removed in an attempt to save the life of that individual. Considering the present state of our dealing with criminals, which is, according to my calculations, not right, I want to go one step further and assume that those sympathetic people would, of course, recommend such an operation to be performed when by chance the patient is a convicted murderer, who is waiting the time of execution, in an attempt to save the life of that murderer, so that the period of waiting on the death row may be continued.

Although in this latter scenario, involving the murderer, the physician and the surgeon ought to perform their best medical and surgical duties, as they are medical practitioners and not the ones in charge of making the decisions related to the crime, but the whole picture seems to be very illogical, according to my reasoning. Those people who are sympathetic towards criminals rationalize the serious and aggressive physical action to be carried out on the patient's body in an effort to save the life of that person. In other words, those sympathetic people justify the very aggressive physical action to be carried out on the murderer in an attempt to save the life of that individual who has been waiting, possibly far too long, on death row, and we are still wasting the society's resources on that person, but the application of severe evident physical punishment in trying to save the future lives of many many many innocent people of our society is considered by them cruel and inappropriate when applied to the criminal who has committed armed robbery, who has killed in cold blood the teller of a bank, or who has murdered the cashier of a store together with other innocent bystanders.

If they broaden the scope of their reasonable thinking, rather than having an emotionally narrow vision, they can see that this treatment is needed to save the lives of many innocent individuals and the future health of the whole society of ours.

By not practicing adequately severe punishments in a timely manner, not only are we unfair to the victims in the vast innocent society, but we are also very cruel to the large number of criminals who are living in misery due to the sequelae of their wrongdoings, while they have had the potentiality of enjoying a normal life, away from commitment of crime, if they had lived in a society with strong rules preventing their first criminal involvement.

In dealing with the murderers, capital punishment, if carried out in a timely and evident manner, seems to be much more logical than life sentence in prison. Also long waiting periods on the death row do not appear right to me. Death sentences for the murderers can be much more deterrent to the other potential criminals, if practiced properly. When the murderer is kept in prison for a long period of time, this is an unnecessary burden and expense for the whole innocent society and also a wrong message to the other potential criminals. If the one who purposely took away the life of an innocent person is supplied, during the term of incarceration, with means of comfort, this would be neither fair to the innocent society, who has to support the facilities, nor a proper lesson to the others. If, to the contrary, the murderer is suffering hardship in the prison, then it is very reasonable to practice proper early execution, to shorten the period of time wasted in keeping that individual in order to educate the society much more correctly and to eliminate, through reduction of crime in our society, the need for so many facilities housing large numbers of inmates.

In an effort to make adequate use of the period of time the criminals are incarcerated, the society should be informed properly of the serious physical and emotional difficulties related to imprisonment for their awareness of what one can expect and would deserve as a consequence of committing crime.

To excuse the criminal with reason of insanity seems to be offering an available potential hiding place to the other criminals. The one who is capable of committing the crime ought to be punished for it unless excused by the victim or the victim's agent. If the person has such a poor mental capability at the time of a committed crime that we consider the individual not to be responsible for the action, then perhaps the ones responsible for having let loose in the society without the needed protection or restraint, such an irresponsible person ought to be tried with adequate punishment. This would be the right education in trying to keep the others from similar actions while discouraging the criminals and their protectors from using this unreasonable excuse to delay or avoid punishment.

For such an important subject it may be justified to have repeated in the last few paragraphs some of the points already mentioned in the earlier pages of this book.

45

Fair or Unfair

Some of us complain about unfairness of life and the injustices of this world. They use the difference in the living standards and the inequality of the amount of available means of comfort for different people as indicators of unfairness in this life. This is not only a useless claim but also a wrong criticism.

If those who criticize this life for unfairness do not believe in the fact that we have a soul with the capacity for making decisions, and they consider us to be only some kind of biochemical robots, then there would be no reason to care about the differences in this world, same as when we are dealing with the inanimate objects and how we treat the pieces and parts of the computers and machines differently. But, if they agree that we each have a soul with true feeling, and the decision making capability which is not just the effect of haphazard nerve currents, and they agree that there is a permanent after-life, then what really matters is the way we try to make use of the present transient life to affect our worthwhile future.

I call the critical comments about the justice of this life useless, as I believe we human beings in this world ought to try seriously to carry out our duties properly. But making a judgment on how the creation, which we are only part of, should have been in any way different from what it is, is clearly beyond our responsibility and obviously above our comprehension. We have not been given the responsibility of evaluating the quality of creation of the world and the life in it, but we are the ones to be judged on our performance. We cannot and should not apply the worldly rationale of our own duties and standards in trying to evaluate the quality of the creation and how this period of life is being managed. While we are instructed to be fair in dealing with others, we cannot compare that to the justice of creation and fairness of life towards the creatures, as we are observing only the surface and making our judgment based on what we can see in this temporary life.

The value of this life, with what we do during this period, is perhaps enormous because of its influence on the quality of our eternal life, but the significance of whatever degree of comfort and joy, or the sufferings and sorrow that we have in this world can be nil when we pay attention to the fact that according to sound mathematics and calculation, the value of this limited period of time we live here, compared to the eternal life which is infinite, would be zero. The true justice with what we receive in the life ahead can be far beyond our present level of understanding.

Those who are critical of our world and life, calling the differences in our living conditions unfair, should be reminded that they cannot suggest or imagine any other alternative that could be fair to their expectation since any minor or major difference would be, to their reasoning, still different degrees of injustice or unfairness towards some of the creatures. They cannot expect the life on earth to be all homogeneous. They cannot expect all of the living beings to be only lions, so that they would not become prey, or all to be rabbits, so that there would be none to prey on them, or all to be pigeons, able to fly, or all to be fish and able to live in the ocean, or all to be unisex mankind of exact same physical and other characteristics with similar living conditions, or all to be only a kind of bacterium or other microorganism, without the possibility of attacking one another or having any chance of causing sickness or becoming infected.

In this temporary life we are being tested on how we perform our part, how properly we fulfill our obligations, and how well we control our desires in spite of the variety of temptations. It seems quite logical that we live in a world with a wide range of diversity. Once we agree that we need to have variety and difference, then we have to accept that we cannot place any limit to the degree of the differences that exist among us so that we would consider them justifiable according to our worldly judgment. If an insect has limited vision while there are birds of prey with high distant visual acuity or animals that can see well at night, if the eagle needs to fly in the search of food while the earth worm lives underground, if there are tiny creatures difficult to be seen with very short life spans, while there are animals that live long, and if we people live in a variety of circumstances and have a wide range of different characteristics and qualities, this is all part of life that we have been given in this world. Since to us it only appears as random possibilities, and we do not quite understand the basis for our being here, nor how we are exactly being tested, we should just accept the life to be perfect for us as it is, since this is all we have, and we try very hard to make use of all of what we have in showing that we want to do our part right.

It is in how we perform our obligations and treat one another or the society that there can be justice and injustice, or fairness and unfairness, with observation of how we human beings can cause different degrees of worldly favor or harm to each other, as individuals or as groups. It is through the observation of the living conditions of our fellow mankind and the behavior of our people, together with the results of the good and bad that we have done to each other that we may learn a lot about how well we are performing as a society. We ought to understand how much we can blame ourselves for the unfavorable living conditions of many, and we should also appreciate our obligations for how we are supposed to offer unselfish service to the society.

While we do not understand how we are being judged finally in view of the wide range of differences we have in this life, and while we ought to try very hard to do our part correctly, so that we may help to improve the living conditions of others and may earn a better status in the life ahead, yet we cannot compare with certainty the people with each other, neither regarding the quality of their person, nor when trying to estimate the collective value of their joy or sadness in life. Our judgment of both, the degree of goodness of another person by observation of the actions, without proper knowledge of the intentions and the level of total pleasures, without knowing what goes on in the mind of that person, can be completely wrong, as it is based on superficial observations.

A comparison of the living conditions of the individuals in this temporary life and the differences thereof cannot be any basis for expression of objection towards life and this world. If we consider living individuals each as a separate being, the life which has been given to each one should be evaluated and considered separately, without comparison with others, since for each of us that is just what we have received, and we are not connected to others in our existence.

If, on the other hand, we are all considered as interrelated parts of the same unit of life on this planet, then while each part is trying to perform correctly, with duties towards the general unit and other parts, there is no objection to the differences that already exist between the different individuals, in the same way that we accept the different conditions of function and qualities or characteristics for the organs and parts of our body without critically objecting that the foot is exposed to much stress of pressure, the colon being in touch with many bacteria, and the nose having to tolerate the changes of temperature. What is important is that the parts carry out their duties right, each being in harmony with what is available and showing proper consideration for the assigned responsibilities.

46

What a Waste It Is

I made a remark elsewhere in the book that my personal feeling is against the spending of money together with people's time and other resources for different political campaigns in excess of what would be needed just for supplying the electing or selecting individuals with the basic information which is required in assisting them towards making their choices with adequate knowledge and fairness. I would like to elaborate further on this subject and insist that the spending of excessive amount of funds by candidates and their supporters is not only a waste, but it can also generate other negative points. It clearly has a detrimental effect on the society's financial well-being because, apart from being an economical loss for the society that ultimately pays the expenses, it also causes a number of other problems such as the examples that follow:

1. There is obvious advantage through this process for the ones who afford to spend more, so there can be better chance of success for the wealthier candidates rather than those who are more suitable for the positions.

2. It may increase the possibility of winning for the one who uses the occasion for negative propaganda, false accusations, and unethical arguments, even to the point of disturbing the society's peace and comfort through annoying discussions and debates during advertisements. As a result of this behavior a very damaging vicious cycle may be formed in relation to the function of the politicians and how properly they serve the society. If among the candidates there exists a better chance of success for those who are wealthier and who have been better supported by rich people, then those candidates, when in the office, may show special support towards the function of their favored rich ones, making them get richer, and then in return they can support them in future campaigns.

Another parallel vicious cycle may be that the candidates for offices would use much of the influence of the broadcasting and news media in their struggle to obtain the votes required for getting them to their desired positions. Then, after getting to the office, they might feel obligated to support those media wholeheartedly in keeping their friendship for future use during later campaigns, rather than doing to them and for all of the mass media what would be to the best interest of everybody and the society's future well-being.

47

The Light and Vision

It seems that the people who belong to different religious groups have generally been advised to perform regular prayers of one kind or another. This, apparently, has been insisted upon as a very strong recommendation. Nevertheless, some individuals do not attend to this important duty of theirs. Some may have the feeling that if they spend time to perform the prayers it would therefore be like doing a favor. They should think properly and realize that God Almighty does not have a need for anybody's favor since God has ultimate power over everything. We are the ones in need of favors and blessings to be bestowed upon us by Our Creator. If the prayer that we perform could be considered a favor, it would be a favor that we do for ourselves and perhaps for the ones for whom or on whose behalf at times we pray. Our ability to pray to God Almighty, by our having received the guidance to do it, is in itself an opportunity.

In our material world, we can perhaps compare this privilege to having the eye that can see and the coming of the visible light to it. Opening of the eye and looking at the world, we are taking advantage of the opportunity of being able to see. If we keep our eyes closed, with the feeling that it is a favor to look and that it requires effort, we will be missing a big opportunity and losing a great available chance of seeing the world with the light and finding the right way to go on. The eye is for the material sight. If we are blessed with having the spiritual eye through the understanding of faith and the need for prayer, then by performing the prayers we are opening our spiritual eye in an effort to see the truth and to be guided in the right path, which sight and seeing are not comparable in value to the material eyesight and looking.

Perhaps among the people who are not accustomed to performing their regular prayers, many of them, while amazed with the temporary luxuries of this world, are very anxious to find an occasion for speaking with or being close to a person of higher worldly authority or one who possesses much wealth or fame, the degree of their joy being dependent on the level of that person's importance or influence. They should, therefore, think and try to understand how privileged we are, if we have the permission of speaking directly to The Highest Authority Of All Being, at such a proximity that our voice can be heard immediately and our thoughts received instantly. What a pity if we do not take proper advantage of such a priceless opportunity in our lives.

48

Those who Deserve and Those who Don't

It seems very reasonable to assume that having cooperation with harmony among the people of our world may result in improvement of the living conditions for all on this planet. By writing this book, I am hoping to generate more friendship among the mass of nicer individuals. I certainly do not want to cause formation of a group separated from the others. I believe we already have too many groups in our society and many unfriendly gaps existing between some of them. I sincerely hope that there will be an increase of friendship and closer association among the already existing groups of mankind. I am writing this book with very high hopes. I hope that many will read it. I hope that a large number of the **better people of the society** of this world will pay attention to some parts which may make sense to them, from what I have written. Then, by looking with a more objective eye at what goes on around them, they may see more clearly what is being done by some members of the society.

I hope that with this clearer understanding there will be more or better unity among these wonderful people all over the world in their efforts to reduce or eliminate the vicious influence of those with evil intentions. I hope that they do not let a minority of selfish individuals among politicians and members of governments of different countries or nations place them against each other with hatred as a way of securing their own positions of power. I hope that they eradicate the wrong influence of the few from the religious leaders and instructors who cause more and more disparity among the good citizens of our world through separation of groups to secure their own sustenance with false emphasis on the superiority of their own groups over others or with wrong presentation and exaggeration of the position of separate idols, in keeping the groups to their own, rather than letting them feel pleasure in true universal unity of faith. I hope that they do not allow the few selfish ones among the responsible individuals in the news media or broadcasting professions and publishing industries sabotage the harmony of the decent life and the proper peaceful progress of our society through their brain-washing of their own nations in different countries or parts of our world against other equally good people. I hope that they strive to get rid of the prejudice and selfishness that can appear in different groups due to persuasions by the extremists and fanatics who lead our groups to more separation with an increase of mutual dislike. I hope that many of the readers of the book may agree with some of the content of this writing and try more vigorously to correct the society. Then it may be possible that through their correct persuasions, while adequately obeying the proper existing laws of their communities and cooperating with the responsible authorities, they can at the same time cause gradual change in the laws and rules towards betterment of the society.

I also hope that many members of the future generations manage to read this book or get to learn properly about its content at a very young age so that they may agree with some of these viewpoints at the early stages of life. Then while growing up they may adapt more to chastity, honesty, self-control, self-sacrifice, and decent human and family values, all under the umbrella of faith or belief in God Almighty, and while following the instructions delivered by the prophets and the advice given by the parents and other benevolent elders.

After all, the major shaping up of our society and the essential corrections in our lifestyles need to be started at the young age of the coming generations since we grown-ups have become accustomed to living in an atmosphere polluted with such a dense concentration of wrongdoing and moral corruption that it would not be easy for many of us to clean up our acts successfully and change our habits properly. Still, we have to try very hard to correct our lifestyles as much as possible and to help our young ones become better people. All of the laws and rules of the nations and the efforts of the governments are not enough on their own to correct our society. The correction has to be started at the level of the individuals that form the society. The young ones must grow up with better principles, so that our society's future may gradually improve. They need to feel content at the very early stages of life while receiving the needed tender affection from their concerned and attentive elders, and to be taught the proper lessons of decent life, so that they grow up with better qualities, learning to differentiate between right and wrong.

They should appreciate the experiences of others in life while following right advice, rather than grow up in the company of devious peers, some of whom can be observed among the adolescents of our present generation, who might behave rebelliously against the manners of the better members of decent conservative society and attempt to differ from them in attire, appearance, and behavior, diverting from the clean norm, in their attempt to please, or to be accepted by, the misbehaving section of our young society.

Our present and future **youth** ought to observe with wise curiosity the behavior of their existing society, then learn to follow the better qualities of others and to refrain from repeating their mistakes. One of the most important principles of social life they should adhere to is the offering of their respect and giving their support to those who try correctly to do good for the society, rather than directly or indirectly helping the wrongdoers who are the source of injuries of one kind or another to the society and its future. These wonderfully talented young minds may learn that our present adult society is suffering seriously from the consequences of a variety of our own mistakes. One of these mistakes is the unwise and inappropriate behavior of the large masses of our very nice people all over the world, on one hand towards each other as groups, and on the other hand towards the extremely small minorities who are in positions of higher influence. They should be enthusiastic to present their support to the people who are trying to do right, and have enough courage to dominate their fears and emotions in keeping from offering their honor and help to the wrongdoers, even if they are in a state of impressive social influence.

We, as part of a worldwide society, are tolerating a tremendous degree of misery as a result of this simple but serious error of offering our **misplaced respect** and honor on one hand and our support and encouragement in many different ways on the other hand to those that we should not. At the same time many of us whose mutual cooperation and proper support with friendship could be very beneficial to the society and its future are careless or even unfriendly towards one another. The large masses of people are, in different aspects of function, under the control of extremely small minorities. There are, among these influential minorities, some individuals with superb human qualities who deserve their position and make very good use of it in serving the society. At the same time, those who lack the required admirable qualities can abuse the privileges granted to them by the society, applying their influence to hurt, rather than help, the majorities. Our misplaced favorable and unfavorable attitudes, with detrimental effects in their applications, can be observed in many aspects of the society's functions. It may be worthwhile to make reference to a few, even if it would be a repetition.

The large masses of productive people struggle to make a living while there are the very **small minorities** of individuals, perhaps mainly functioning in more urban areas of this world, who are in worthless activities but successful enough to live comfortably at the expense of the efforts of others. Still these useless parasites are honored by the masses, who are easily impressed by wealth and luxury, instead of caring about the quality of the person. Some people, who complain about their financial problems, may still spend money in doing what can hurt their mind and body, as they give in to their desires. These people, through what they do, are often supporting and encouraging to those who prepare and sell the means of attractive but useless or harmful entertainment. It is the productive but poor person helping the nonproductive but wealthy to get richer. Then, many continue to respect the same rich ones for what they have. The average people who constitute the very large mass of the society have to show clearly that there are encouragement and honor in the society for people of better quality and definitely not for wealth or glamour.

The very large majority from the mass of a society may suffer continuously from financial hardship. Yet, they may subconsciously respect and, through their behavior in the social functions, support the very small minority which is in control of most of the society's wealth although among these exceedingly wealthy people there may be the ones who do not deserve that support. Some of these extra-rich individuals may not be enjoying their lives and suffer from complications of having too much, but still struggling to increase the quantity as much as possible and to keep it out of the reach of those who may need it desperately.

The young and old of our society can be hurt in the long run by the productions of some of the members of the news **media** and other broadcasting, publishing, and entertaining industries. Still, the members of the very same society that is hurt by them, support them, watching their harmful but attractive presentations and buying or using their variety of products. It is obvious though, that if the mass of people cooperates in boycotting what is harmful, by way of discouraging the few selfish individuals who are included in those professions, there would be better chance for improvement of the quality of decent services of their other more morally-inclined colleagues, with opportunity for greater success in preparation and presentation of their useful products.

In the present state of mankind's civilization, we may sense the possibility of having in many small communities, towns, and cities, a few people, who are tied together with **invisible connections** and are holding political, financial, legal, and other controlling powers over the mass of people. In some bigger communities and populations the same possibility may be felt to exist on a much larger scale. The majorities may be oppressed to the point that they may not dare to oppose the members of the small influential group, even when they indulge in serious wrongdoing.

When someone from the average majority, whose right has been abused or violated, becomes brave enough to take effective action against one of the powerful few, not only may the whole system be manipulated against the innocent victim, but a great number of people may also be skeptical in supporting the case, as they would be hesitant to oppose the influential. This, can be seen in many parts of the world, regardless of the systems of government in place and the political status there.

Although in any of these communities, the few in control who may be abusing their positions of power, are using the collective force of the whole community to keep them strong, the mass of people, whose support is being abused against their own group, are feeling weak, as they are not united together except in supporting and respecting those few influential individuals who enjoy authority and luxurious living. If my suspicion is correct and this condition does exist in some places on earth, then in those communities the mass of population may continuously tolerate problems in their daily activities, causing constant unnecessary stress and at times acute augmentation of the degree of the stress for some innocent members of their community, resulting in ongoing damage to the society and its function.

The large majority of innocent people living in this world are almost continuously suffering from financial, physical, emotional, and other losses, due to the actions of a minority of **criminals and wrongdoers**. Crimes of varying degrees, with their related aspects of damage to the society, cause very serious problems, more or less in every part of the world. We are also losing much of the society's advantages and resources through a variety of other wrongdoings. Still, many from the innocent majority, who are suffering from such losses, demonstrate sympathy for the criminals, rather than towards the victims, interfering with severe and swift physical punishment that should be applied towards the criminals by way of educating the society. Even in the face of their misbehaviors, the innocent majority that ignores many kinds of wrongdoing may honor and support the individuals for their achievements at times in totally useless areas. They pay attention to wealth and glamour, to power and authority, to fame and what could make news, such as success in sports and competitions or daring performances and many other activities, to the degree that they may completely forget or ignore the harm being done by the same individual. They forgive the guilt out of being impressed emotionally by some achievements.

Still, the variety of whatever harm is done can hurt the society, no matter who is doing it and at what status. Some may abuse public funds for personal use. Some may be involved in bribery and misguided application of their influence. Some may be involved with the abuse of drugs and drinking of alcohol. Some may harass others at the work place or in public in different ways. Some may deceive others, stealing their resources. Some may tell lies in a court of law or elsewhere. Some may be unfaithful in different capacities. Some may cheat their clientele in business or may knowingly present defective products at work. There are so many ways through which our wrongdoings can ultimately hurt the society, and yet the majority of nice people of the society often shies away from objecting effectively to those who are committing them.

The large and small gatherings of people who are grouped together for a variety of reasons may at times be under the **misguidance** and inappropriate influence of wrong individuals who are in positions of control and authority in some groups. Still, on many occasions the members of the group may ignore the wrongdoings of figures in authority and give them their support and vote of confidence because of emotional and unhealthy attachments or out of individual weakness when facing dominant characters. The group may be supporting the leaders who act with superiority and arrogance even with their own people. Many a time some of the leaders can generate trouble and dislike between their group and others or among the factions of the very same group that they lead, to secure their own position of influence with its accompanying privileges.

In every part of the vast surface of this planet, among the many who live on it, regardless of their skin color, nationality, the language they speak, or the religious group they belong to, we may find people with wonderful human qualities. But there are also, in almost every corner of this great land some efforts spent by a few, either due to their ignorance or through their selfishness, to **divide and subdivide** these wonderful people into groups, for a variety of excuses and under different names, then to feed each group large doses of prejudice, generating and increasing dislike and hate between them and other groups that may include many equally nice people. They may even stimulate serious hateful interactions and reactions between the groups, through which there may be ongoing acceleration of unfriendly relationships, with many nice people hating and hurting one another out of such deliberate sabotage initiated by a few unwise and selfish individuals.

Once some aggressive, unfriendly interactions have taken place between the groups, then there can be appearance of so much irrational dislike that any attempt to offer a reasonable solution to the problem may not easily work to clear the rage, even in the eyes of the very nice and wise people of the opposite sides, as they have been hurt. The society as a whole, not only suffers from missing the priceless beneficial outcomes of a friendly cooperation which are absent between those groups, but also suffers tremendous financial and other losses because of those groups' injurious interactions due to the misguided influences since any loss is ultimately a deficit for the society in general to tolerate.

Our youth should be educated properly with the kind of broad education which is needed to help them be better human beings, so that there will be improvement of the quality of life on earth, so the coming generations would be better than we are and live more wisely. The mass of people, who grow up with the right principles and correct education, may cooperate to cleanse the society as much as possible from a variety of problems that we have been facing, some of which were mentioned in the few preceding paragraphs. Through their dedication in doing what they feel is right, rather than following their passion and desires, with adequate knowledge and strong will to perform correctly, not only that they may succeed more and more in counteracting the detrimental effects of a small selfish minority who may want to oppress the majority and take advantage of them for their own sake, but also, after adequate cleansing of the atmosphere of life on this planet and having fewer selfish people and a larger number of better educated ones in the society, there may come a time when there will be proper scarceness of the abusers who look for ways of hurting the masses for their own advantage.

This may be possible when members of the society of mankind in this world become so nicely educated that they would appreciate the true pleasures of life, which are beyond what money can buy and are not necessarily available to everyone who controls abundance of wealth or influence. The wise people who constitute that society will not even attempt to hurt or oppress others for the sake of selfish financial or similar gains. On the one hand they would appreciate standards and goals to reach in life which are much higher than the temporary material privileges. On the other hand, in that adequately progressive society, with mutual cooperation, their lives could be generally filled with so much contentment, that they would not need any more to get through selfish acts in those communities that truly cooperate together in using their mutual efforts as much as possible in preparing a better life for all. A society so educated could put abusers out of function when people of understanding recognize them easily and do not tolerate their harmful activities.

It may take generations to wipe the society out of the vicious minority who are among the many influential and authoritative figures of our world. Those who are so selfish that for the wasted glamour of their own life and the supply of luxury for a few surrounding them, could cause serious misery with famine, sickness, injury, and death to vast numbers of innocents. Yet they do not have the human feelings to understand the real consequences of their actions, nor can they change easily to a normal, honest, and decent way of living. In different parts of the world, many of the ones who possess much authority are somehow restricted, due to their status, from doing a lot of ordinary outside activities freely. It appears as if they are confining themselves in their extravagant positions, with much effort being spent by the ones responsible to preparing and maintaining their limitations as if they are living in a golden cage, in which some of them struggle to stay as they cannot imagine being happy out of it, or they feel insecure without it.

There are a few among them who have wicked and selfish intentions. These few may disturb, from inside the cage, the peace and rest of the outside world, and when they get the chance, they may hurt each other or cause trouble for any nice person who is with them in the cage, while they are on their own part often suffering from mental anguish and a lot of stress. Nevertheless, they are deprived from having access to, and are unable to appreciate, the beauty of a life with peaceful conscience in clean freedom away from their golden cage. They cannot be easily persuaded to learn the lessons of life from their benevolent friends who are in similar capacities, entrusted with much authority or in control of abundant wealth while they continue to be very concerned about the people, keep their human qualities with comfortable conscience, have proper ethics, and follow decent family and social values. They help and support others who are in need and are not only trying to collect as much of worldly treasures or possibilities as they can for themselves and their close ones. They enjoy life without arrogance and free from too much of wasteful and restrictive superficial luxuries.

The major correction of our society has to be started by our very young generation so that they grow up with better attitude and behavior towards different aspects of life for self and for others. They should try to correct our mistakes, looking forward to a better future. Our present society is, generally in a bad shape and is getting worse, too. We are noticing more problems with crime, disruption of family values, and breaking down of the rules of humanity, especially in the more crowded and larger cities, with our becoming almost as parts of a machine, working with less and less of human feelings for each other. The more urban the place is where we live in, the more selfishness and stress we may observe, and the less affection and sincere friendship among the people.

At the same time, we are approaching an overpopulated world, replacing the trees with houses and changing fertile lands into residential areas, the small towns growing larger and becoming bigger cities, with almost unavoidable increase in a variety of pollutions and faster deterioration of the quality of life. Then the big cities and larger communities export their corruption to others who may still be living with clean principles, which we may find at higher proportions in smaller communities. It is essential that the generations grow up with such a human attitude and conscience that they feel hurt and uncomfortable deep inside when doing something wrong for themselves or especially to others. It is essential that during the many years of proper education of youth, groups of people of any capacity who feel comfortable in themselves when they cause to hurt, bother, injure, or kill the innocents in different ways, are gradually replaced by those whose capable conscience, strong beliefs, and decent principles support them in avoiding such an act and in effectively disapproving of such actions.

We grown-ups of the corrupted society hurt each other directly or cause one another's distress indirectly, often without noticing the untoward effects of what we do, at times aware of the result but making excuses to comfort our conscience. Some of us may become accustomed to doing seriously wrong things, ignoring the vetoes of our weak conscience. Often the wrongdoers do not pay attention to the outcomes of their wrong acts but, as we often do, look with an objective eye at the mistakes of others. What they do to others without feeling the pain is not what they would like to be done to them.

We can observe multifarious injustices, unfair dealings, crimes with degrees of seriousness, discriminations, oppressions, dishonesty, breaking of promises, variety of harassments, and many other means of hurting one another, yet on each occasion those who do the wrong usually do not feel self-conscious objections to their misdeeds; hence, they do not try properly to stop their own misbehaviors. But another observer may appreciate the lack of wisdom in their acts.

When groups or gangs of young individuals are involved in a serious act as one group may cause injury and damage to the members of their opponents, the wiser adult community would consider this action unfounded, uncivilized, and a source of increase of stress for the community to which they all belong. They feel this kind of unwise aggression would hurt the harmony of life and disturb the constructive cooperation that is expected from all of the members of that community and is needed for their progress, stability, and peace of mind. Yet, the members of the gangs who are involved with these violent behaviors do not think wisely to overcome their combative emotions with sensible reasoning and honest logic so that they encourage themselves and their friends to stop their misbehaviors.

While we members of the adult society can see their mistakes with our critical eyes, considering the groups or gangs of youth who belong to the same community, live in one city, or have the same nationality, or whatever unifying characteristics, unwise in having aggressive and damaging behavior towards each other, how could we possibly rationalize our own behavior of forming groups all over the world with a variety of excuses, then spending massive volumes of resources of this planet to build up what is required to hurt each other's groups more acutely while every group claims innocence of self and guilt for the opponents. Perhaps a wise observer would consider these actions unwise and all of our groups generally emotional and selfish, in the same way that we may judge the young groups and gangs, but on a much larger scale. Although the surface of earth is large enough for us to live on it, we may have the capability of ruining it if we continue to reproduce out of control and, while disregarding our admirable human values, we fight and hurt one another in the struggle towards competition for survival. That could be the destruction of the magnificent life on earth.

49

Why this Book was Written

This book is not written by a sociologist. All I have done is to point out here some of the problems that can be observed in our society by just looking attentively. It is not a religious book, nor am I knowledgeable enough to elaborate on religious instructions, but only to emphasize the fact that there is only One Supreme Authority as The Creator Of All Being, so there should be one religion for all of us to which we belong in unity. It is not a racial book, in honor of one race against others, but shows that we ought to have no recognition of race in a manner that results in discrimination when offering any kind of respect or privilege. It is not a political writing, in support of one nation or country and the use of its unclean selfish politics against another one, but to declare that we have to feel as one nation on the surface of this planet if we want to try to save it from early decay.

To attain global unity among the better people, which is required for achieving success in the fight against the deleterious actions of wicked minds, it would be reasonable to expect that these understanding persons should try to eradicate, as well as possible, the disuniting factors that interfere with the intimate friendship of their groups. These wonderful people, who are less selfish and care about others and about the future well-being of the whole society, ought to try very hard to get rid of unwise prejudices that their individuals or groups may have towards one another by sincerely focusing on the human qualities of others and their intentions. This ought to be achieved without positive or negative group prejudices, or favoritism or antagonism, or categorization or stereotyping of other people simply on the basis of their group attachments. They should realize that any of us might have some strong feelings or beliefs, depending on our living conditions and the circumstances around us. They should also keep in mind that we could possibly have some belief or behavior completely different from what we are used to, if we did have the needed exposure to that, or had grown up among those accustomed to it, even if at our present state of mind we may be critical of it.

They must then do two things to correct this potential problem of our society:

1. They have to try to control their feeling of criticizing other righteous people simply on the basis of their differences, unless there are adequate unbiased thinking and proper justification, so that they treat others, as individuals or groups, with fairness, just as they expect to be treated by others.

2. The second very important action is that they should apply strong effort towards eliminating a variety of factors which are placing groups of good citizens of our world against each other. In this regard, there are many areas of group attachments which are a source of separation and often unwise opposition of considerate persons against each other due to conflict of interests.

These better individuals of our society all over the world must deliberately refrain from letting their group loyalty interfere with the more important responsibility of theirs which is towards supporting the whole society. If there are divisions because of nationality or living in different parts of the world, still the inhabitants of each location should try to recognize and respect the rights of others to the point that they do not get involved in being a source of unfair harm to any other group to ensure the security of their own. As a consequence, they would help to improve the life of all of the groups with the feeling of being part of a larger family.

While there exist differences among us related to our physical characteristics, we must comprehend the fact that these differences of skin color or other particulars cannot and should not be a source of assigning superiority or inferiority to the groups, nor should they cause one group's unjust feeling or the presentation of dislike in any degree towards another group. We ought to appreciate that we all are part of the human race living in this world. This global unity cemented by cooperation, is a must, although in spite of such a cooperation the correction of serious problems of our society may still require the time of a few generations.

A very powerful element of unity or separation of our groups may be related to faith or religious affiliations. The better citizens of our world, who perhaps carry much greater supply of this quality of being religious, should make proper use of it for promoting the unity of mankind. This may be appropriately done if all of these individuals who believe in the existence of The Creator Of All Being insist on this most valuable unifying understanding while disregarding the unimportant, but disuniting particulars attached to their faith. To fill the separating gaps between their groups, these nicer individuals around the world should insist on worshipping The One Almighty God while they spend deliberate effort to eliminate the causes of disparity. At the same time that we appreciate with admiration the whole creation of this world and accept that every force or energy has its origin in and from The Creator Of All, we should carefully refrain from incorporating any portion of the creation, whether with human face or other animate or inanimate qualities, so directly with The Creator that we make the mistake of worshipping that material appearance in this world as part of The Creator or considering partnership for The Supreme Authority.

If the people of different cultures, while speaking their different languages, are calling The Creator by different names, they should still realize clearly that they all are referring to The Same One Lord Of All Being. At the times that we are praying and speaking to The Creator, we should remember that while we may be looking at a direction, we are not worshipping the material objects of whatever kind existing in that direction or in front of us, but only The Creator Of All, The One Supreme Authority, The Lord Of All Being, God Almighty. This unifying common belief can become a strong bond of friendship, resulting in more and more of sincere cooperation and mutual assistance among the groups, as long as they all insist on the same belief, without the groups' claiming superiority over others because of certain distinguishing characteristics of their faith, without each group selecting or insisting on the importance of a separate religious figure or prophet in comparison with others, and without the members of each group unjustly stereotyping the members of another group or groups collectively with ill remarks.

If this correction is not done, it is easy to envision the future of the people on earth fraught with disparities, with continuation of aggression among them, each group trying, through different approaches, to gain control of others, or to prove superiority over their groups, with the hope of future triumph. If, instead of each group's emphasizing the importance of its selection with repeated reference to one chosen person, character, prophet, or idol, they all insist on believing in and worshipping The One And Only, The Supreme Being, without each separate group assigning to The Creator different qualities of their choice, and if the groups respect with honor the prophets and messengers who brought the message for us from God Almighty, while avoiding comparison of their degree or level of importance, leaving that judgment or comparison to The Highest Knowledgeable Authority, then the people of the world could perhaps be on the right track towards religious unity.

This needs to be done by us at the level of the mass of the people everywhere. We cannot expect the teachers of religion and the religious authorities to be able to perform such a challenging task on their own. It requires the perseverance and dedication of the members of the society in general, the same as would be true for establishment of other group friendships. The leaders, whether religious, political, racial, or in other groups, possibly have among them individuals who may insist on the importance of the separate distinguishing elements, emphasizing the righteousness and deserving superiority of their own groups, trying to continue the separations in the struggle to keep their own authority with its accompanying privileges.

Some authoritative figures may even have the belief that through the separation or the lack of friendly unity of the people, they can retain a more secure position of control and power over them. But among the authorities, as would be true for any other group of individuals, there exist different degrees of human qualities. If the people's opinion and determination lean strongly towards the direction of taking proper action in doing what is right towards improving the world for everybody, they will probably receive adequate support from the more benevolent of their leaders.

50

A Time that should be Appreciated

During the years of our living in this world, we pass through different stages of life, with their related physiological and other characteristics. Each age or period of our life should be appreciated for itself. Since going through these stages is normal for us, we generally have to avoid the expression of an attitude of dislike towards any of them. Although we do not approve of a grown-up habitually behaving like a child, nor do we like to have at our young age some of the functional impairments that the bodies of the very old persons are accustomed to, we have to accept each period for itself with contentment, and at whichever stage of life we are, we should try to make good use of it happily and correctly.

The normal and adequate growth of a child should not be admired with exaggeration to the point that the child becomes too enthusiastic to grow up, does not appreciate the period of very young age, and rushes to reach adolescence, or does, inappropriately, what the adults do, with a sense of hurriedness for appearing more like them. Nor should we talk about old age so critically that we fear approaching it, or after reaching it instead of appreciating the advantages that we have, we waste our time in grief for what we could be missing.

Since during life, from the days of childhood and beyond, we are all the time advancing gradually toward old age, it seems sensible to insist that we should try at every stage of this life to look forward to that latter period of it with optimism and confidence. Those who are looking forward, expecting the future with anxiety and happiness, can enjoy their lives, as they know that the future is coming. Those who are afraid of the future and prefer a state of standstill without advancing in age are deeply sad inside, even though they may be having good times intermittently.

We ought to enjoy life by living right and doing good to others, looking forward to old age as the time of having fewer responsibilities, still embracing extra advantages and privileges, expecting to be looked after as needed. During the earlier years of our life we should enjoy offering our financial and other assistance as appropriate, with the confidence that in old age we would have fewer needs, as we would not be expected to work hard and we would be looked after by the society. This is healthier than the attitude that the whole society would be overly money-conscious, struggling to save for the possible difficult older years. Everybody would be worried about the distant future without enjoying the present time properly nor doing what is right for others, passing a stressful life full of worry for old age, taking selfish advantage of the society in the struggle to satisfy that inappropriate concern.

It seems improper that a society, while offering a compliment and in trying to comfort them, addresses the old persons as being young. They may even refer to some aged one as being young at heart. No matter how we are or how we feel, our age is what it is. It is possible that some parts of our body are healthier and some sicker than the average for that age, but still they have the same age. We should not relate what we do not like such as illnesses, with a negative attitude, as definite attachments to a particular stage of life. There are some disabilities and ailments seen often with old age. Those who are anxiously welcoming the period of senior years may think of those as part of the price to pay for such a wonderful opportunity.

Whenever we struggle harder and longer for reaching an occasion, its arrival can be more appreciated and pleasant. If instead of the years of study and passing through the many difficult tests, one could get a college diploma with ease in a very short time, the graduation probably would not be accompanied with so much joy. After striving a lifetime to reach old age, that latter time of living in this world, for the one who has been anxiously looking forward to its arrival, can be wonderfully pleasant. To that person, the possible difficulties and sufferings that may come with old age are like the thorns we can expect to accompany a well-appreciated beautiful rose.

While there are many families who take care of their elders with respect and dignity and demonstration of affection at home or in other suitable facilities, there are some in society that instead of supporting old people with what keeps them happy, encouraged with some pleasant attachment to the community, and letting them go at the time they should, they treat the old as being useless. Then they try, by forcing medical and other care, to elongate that period of rejected seclusion in the struggle to make some old ones remain longer and longer in that final waiting state which can be void of the well-desired and affectionate attachments and performance of useful functions. This may indirectly hurt the society and directly increase the hardship and suffering even for those who were happy with the arrival of old age and have been looking forward with contentment to its termination. It is like having some passengers who have anxiously spent effort in packing their suitcases and have gone through the difficulties of preparing for a well-desired trip. Then, while they are looking forward with pleasure to their leaving, we let them get to the airport or train station, and while they stay there with some difficulties, we keep on postponing their departure.

51

The Well-educated Society

There exist many systems of government in different nations and countries of our society. I am not a politician, nor do I have much knowledge about how those systems function, but I personally feel that it is not the type of regime or system of government that determines the future of a nation and a society, but what greatly matters is the quality of the people of that society. Whatever kind of democratic system is in force, if the people let corruptions of different kinds pollute their society, they will face deterioration in the quality of life with increase of stress and hardship for the average of their people, resulting in diminution of the peace of mind and comfort of the populace.

Their coming generations will then inherit from the predecessors large doses of misery, that would be augmented in size and passed on to their descendants. Then, even the way their government is running can be seriously influenced since the individuals who hold positions of power are none but members of the same society, who may be affected by the same corruptions, and perhaps succeed, with the cooperation of other deviated peers, to function not in line with the democracy or to the advantage of the majority, but to reinforce their own strongholds while searching for clever techniques of oppressing their nations. The principles of democracy and majority rule can then be abused.

In fact, in an attempt to reduce the deleterious effect of emotional decisions and mistakes, we should not ask the opinion of the majority on every item. The majority of a populace can designate suitable individuals and groups to carry out proper assigned responsibilities in the society. Those people are then to make decisions with their expertise and specialties, conscientiously according to what will be right for the society in the long run and not only to satisfy the temporary desires of any group or majority.

When the people of a society are generally determined to do what is right, are faithful, adequately educated, brave and honest, and united together in their efforts towards betterment of their society, no matter what kind of dictatorial government is in force, they can still influence and gradually cleanse their society, including the political functions, from default and pursue their benevolent intentions. I cannot overemphasize the importance of proper education of the young and the whole society as a key factor towards achieving this goal.

52

Duty and Performance

Discussing pride and what we can be proud of makes me have some feelings that at times may be somehow controversial. We show pride in our race, country of origin, or similar particulars. This does not make sense to me since that kind of happening is out of our control, so we cannot claim any credit for it. Some people may say that they are proud of their ancestors who had much authority and positions of power or they were wealthy, but this is not at all important because it is not the amount of goods they had in their control that counts, but rather how much good they did with it for their society. Even if we express our pride in the good that our parents did, or in the academic and other successes that our children have had, since these are their achievements, they are not to our credit to be proud of. If we have done something which is above and beyond the normal or usual successes of others, still we should consider whether that is an achievement which is exceptional only in impressing others, or that it is truly valuable in the direction of performing service to a society.

So, I am left with the feeling that we cannot demonstrate pride for anything unless we have personally spent some effort of high value in doing something proper and useful for a society and its future. Then on that occasion, still we may debate that perhaps the expression of pride in our own performance could be considered self-admiration with some degree of arrogance, or that we have forgotten that being good and doing what is right is our duty. Therefore, the performance of a duty cannot be a basis for showing pride. Appropriately we should then be pleased and thankful for the opportunity of having had the occasion for doing what we did, for the ability of trying something in the right direction, and for all of the available factors that helped our success.

53

The Final Value of Available Joy

I almost wish I were a mathematician, so that I could possibly express my feelings regarding the supply of pleasure in our society with calculations, and that I could show it better on paper in the form of graphs and diagrams. Still, I will try to write briefly about the subject, although these paragraphs will partly be a repetition of what I have written in some earlier pages.

We are all concerned about our degree of pleasure in life. At every moment we like to be pleased for that instant, and also we want to secure adequate pleasure for our future. The knowledge about the availability of adequate supply of pleasure for the future can itself increase the volume of pleasure of the present moment. Some people pay much attention only to their short-range future pleasure, but some others are more concerned about the future adequacy of their long-range supply, in that they even sacrifice some of the near future pleasures for the sake of increasing the availability of their supply later. But since the feeling of having the security of long-range future pleasure gives, by itself, satisfaction to the latter group, this causes an increase in their supply of pleasure for the moment as well as for the near future. On the other hand, some people pay too much attention to their pleasure of the present and immediate future, ignoring the fact that for having a small volume of some of the present pleasures they will be losing a much larger amount of the same later. In other words, some people forget to take into consideration the total value of the pleasure of their lifetime.

Of the long-range planners, those who believe in the hereafter try to save adequately for that permanent pleasure of the future. They may benefit from an escalating supply of pleasure during this life. This is because they expect the value of that pleasure beyond material life to be much greater, so its expectation can generate in this life tremendous pleasure for them. There are people who sacrifice some amount of their own pleasure in order to increase the pleasure of others. In doing this, they usually cause greater increase of pleasure for others than what they sacrifice of their own. Besides, through the process of donation of that pleasure they generate some new pleasure for themselves as a result of the satisfaction they get from good deeds. Often this increase of the total value of pleasure in a society can be of a large scale, depending on the quality and quantity of the efforts spent. In contrast to this, there are some people who may have the tendency of trying to increase their supply of pleasure at the expense of reducing the pleasure of others, at times inducing severe damage to the pleasure of large masses of people.

This latter state of affairs often causes marked decline in the total value of the society's pleasure since the damage that these people cause to the pleasure of others is usually far greater than the amount of their own gain. The result is severe injury to the life of mankind on earth. There are many examples occurring all over the world where some individuals or groups, while satisfying their own desires and pleasures, which may not even be of much lasting quality, cause tremendous reduction in the pleasure of others, thereby reducing the total value of pleasure of the whole society. There are also great losses caused by their actions indirectly, for example, through the fear that the potential victims have from future disturbances, and the efforts and resources that they spend in the way of prevention and for their own protection. Ultimately, this reduction has, more or less, detrimental influence on the average degree of pleasure in life for all on the planet, including those who are more responsible for this decline and their present and future dear ones, who are and will be living on earth.

54

cA Dreamland

Far away, in the midst of my deep thoughts and wishful imaginations, there exists a dreamland. I like to consider the possibility that someday in the future, somewhere on this planet, some of the descendants of our generation will have the opportunity of living in a place with qualities close to my dreamland.

In my dreamland people live as a society with the feeling of being attached or bonded together with a two-way concern. Each member of the society is concerned about the others in the least selfish manner, while feeling secure and having confidence that the people of their society are also sincerely concerned about that person. In this way, the people of my dreamland have a continuous factor of concern in effect like the gravitational pull that can keep the large mass and small particles together through a two-way attraction, resulting in an adequate supply of confidence, support, trust, and friendship.

The individuals of that land do not feel any need for being selfish, as they already have the concern and support of others in the society. They truly appreciate the fact that for having adequate and continuous supply of the above-mentioned mutual concern, the correct attitude of each person and the whole society towards each other is a common social necessity, with each individual's believing that being nice to others, with honesty and fairness, is everybody's duty without expectation of a compensation or reward from them. The society, at the same time, clearly shows that members who have more concern for the betterment of life of the whole society are favored and supported by the mass of the people.

In that land, there is abundance of wealth and much economic stability since there is a minimum of waste of the assets, and they have more than enough supplies through the very adequate production by people who enjoy what they do, who perform the right work, and who try to do their best. The people are well-supplied with their basic needs. The population is kept close to optimum through proper family planning. As the society is productive and not wasteful, there is abundance of supplies and necessities for all, so the people do the work as they please. Although they work generally hard, they enjoy what they do since individuals choose their business or profession according to their talent and preference. With their deep sense of cooperative obligations and their joy in doing what is right for all, even the amount of effort that they spend with pleasure in performing the work that they like to do is far above the society's general need.

People there are occupied in productive businesses and professions. They are encouraged by the society to continue doing what is considered true service, while they are seriously discouraged from involvement in the occupations which aim at personal gains, at the expense of possible moral, financial, physical, emotional or other damage to the others, or doing the work that can be in conflict with the society's future wellbeing. Since the whole society performs nicely, while working individually and collectively well, enjoying what they do, trying to be positively productive, wasting as little as possible, avoiding useless and harmful activities, and managing their resources properly; there is much supply of the necessities for all of the people, so each working individual is compensated very satisfactorily for the time and effort spent at work.

Hence, each person does not need to work harder or longer than desired, and there is plenty of free time for the people to spend in other activities. As there are fewer hours needed for work, both spouses do not need to be busy away from home. Parents can have more time with children, rather than having to spend their time at work and leaving the children to grow up without adequate concern and loving supervision. Many mothers can attend to the requirements of the home, especially when they have very young children. Families have more time to spend together in group activities and healthy recreation. They also have time to spend in the care of their elders, rather than having to leave them in seclusion and being too busy to give them the affection that they need.

Such people are very careful in using what they earn in the right way and enjoying a healthy life, rather than spending their time and money in wrongdoing, causing ultimate harm to self or others or wasting what they have without careful consideration to the point of unnecessarily having a feeling of inadequacy.

In my dreamland advertisements are for information and introduction of the products and services. There the people do not waste their time or finances towards negative commercials, nor the society's resources in having competitive businesses which are wasteful and not needed. They are so conscientious about their work that competition is not required for making them improve the quality of their product and services, nor for keeping the prices down.

The individuals of that land are so unselfishly concerned about the well-being of the whole society that they want the good life for all. They often would like to leave what is better for others. For example, when a group of people is buying some fruit from the same pile in a market, each of them does not choose the better ones for self, but a random selection, or even leaving the better ones for others who are buying as well. And people who are engaged in business or trade try to pass on their profits, beyond what is required for their comfortable sustenance, to clientele and customers or to charitable budgets of their communities.

In my dreamland the people who are rich voluntarily donate as they can afford to the budget of the society and to the occasional needy who may have to spend, for some reason, more than what is available. There is no need for each person to collect and save a lot of money for self or for the children's future education since everybody is confident that in their well-supplied society their future is expected to be secure and the proper means easily accessible for the education of the young and the care of the disabled and the occasional unattended old people.

There is no incentive in that land for struggling to become excessively wealthy. The people already have more than their basic necessities and are doing the work that they like to do. They are bright and educated so well that they do not enjoy wasting their time or excessive amount of finances in useless activities or wrongdoing. They have been raised in such wonderful families and society that they feel deep in their hearts the concern for the comfort of others. They are so understanding that instead of spending much wealth to buy extravagance for themselves, they enjoy helping to improve the living conditions of others. Besides, the society would not offer any respect or special recognition just for wealth or position of influence, but for better human qualities and for how well a person uses money and power. In fact, the luxury per se and the wealth, void of proper application, bring with them disrespect and dishonor for their owners in that land.

The people of my dreamland promote games of performance, instead of games of chance. They do not make money through participation in the preparation or by playing of games of chance. They do not have locations for the young or old persons to gather, spending their time in wrongdoing with immoral behavior. The places are non-existent, where, in the name of entertainment, some are engaged in playing the games of chance, some waste their time by listening to a loud music while they jump up and down indecently to the crazy rhythm of that ear-hurting sound, and later some of them possibly use addictive substances, and when they have lost their self-control they might get involved in doing other more serious and harmful acts.

Members of that society try to live wisely, functioning sensibly, not only per emotion and desires. At the same time in their interactions with each other they show and feel affections rather than behave like senseless robots. They behave as concerned persons, not as emotionless parts of a big machine. The individuals who have positions of influence and those who face large numbers of people at their work treat them with humility, with an expression of genuine concern and sincerity, not with an attitude of only wanting to get the job done and be successful in the business. In fact, the people of that land are generally nice and treat each other with kindness and appropriate affection. They realize that being nice to others does not cost anything and can help to reduce the stress and increase the joy and productivity of the society, as long as this quality of being nice is not abused by some nor misunderstood or taken advantage of by others.

In that land the people generally try to be good in different aspects of social life. They don't only try to correct their own performance, but are also very concerned about how others act in improving the future for all. They present appropriate criticism towards moral and other misconducts, showing intolerance rather than carelessness towards the personal qualities or behaviors which are clearly in conflict with the future well-being of the society. In doing that, they try aggressively to encourage members of the society to persist in doing what is reasonably right for the sake of all, and they discourage them from submitting to wrongdoing while obviously they strive towards always setting through their own performance the correct example of the same behavior that they preach.

They believe that this concern about the behavior of others in the society and the correct approach to influence their attitude towards their duties and performance in private and public is a must. They know that if we present and apply this kind of concern only towards our close and dear ones and not in dealing with others in the society, by using the excuse that it would be interfering in other people's personal lives, then this could mean that we have all of our love or affection only for our very close ones, whom we do not deprive from our continuous care, advice, and expression of opinion on the right and wrong that they do, and that we are not feeling responsible or even concerned about the characters of other members of the society to which we all belong, forgetting that we are all together a large family on this planet.

The people of that land realize that, while they present their concern and assistance towards others in preventing them from doing wrong and convincing them to do what is right, they expect the people to be different, with many variations of characteristics which are not contradictory to the well-being of the society. Hence, those people would not aim for having a homogeneous society. They also remember that while the responsibility for improvement of others in the society is a must, we ought to try, very carefully and without bias, to have in our minds the fact that more often than not we may be in error when we are critical of other people; therefore, we should let our discussions or debates have a fair bilateral corrective influence rather than remain accustomed to insisting with prejudice on our own thoughts, habits, and expectations to be the only right way.

Individuals with high moral qualities, who constitute the great majority of the people of that land, are united together.

They aggressively show the dominance of the better classes of the society and are sufficiently vocal rather than passive and do not behave as the slaves of any potentially oppressive minority that may like to take advantage of the society by abusing wealth and worldly power.

There is an adequate supply of happiness in my dreamland. As people pay more attention to the future than to the present and since each individual is more concerned about the betterment of living conditions for others than for self, it should be easy to calculate and conclude that, with the generation and preservation of a large bank of joy through the cooperation of the people and without causing any unhappy circumstances for each other, there would clearly be a great supply of total value of pleasure. And since, without wasting, that total amount is all divided among the members of that society, each individual in that land is expected on average to have a much larger supply of happiness throughout life. People are concerned about the quality of their pleasure. They enjoy doing what is right for the future of all, rather than having short-lasting enjoyment for self, from doing what can later cause sadness for them or complications for others.

In that land people do not get engaged in the production or distribution of materials which are considered to be harmful if used by the society, such as tobacco, alcoholic beverages, and addictive drugs other than for medical purposes. They do not get involved in the manufacture, preparation, or sale of a variety of recordings, printed materials, or other items which are not in harmony with the well-being of the society and contain pictures and scenes, or subjects and discussions, that can be considered harmful rather than beneficial. They do not get involved with the tools of gambling, or other items and products and even any toys that, when used, are detrimental to the future well-being of the society and the lasting happiness of its members. Those people do not misuse their financial support for purchase of harmful products or by spending money to watch the wrong performances.

The news media and means of broadcasting or tools of public information, the books and other publications, all present to the society the encouraging aspects and scenes of the wonderful life, promoting the pleasure derived from living decently and doing what is right for self and others. They strive to reinforce the family values with the strength of the bond and mutual faithfulness among the family members. They do not present any product or programs that can be against the ethical and moral values or safety of the society and detrimental to its future well-being, not preparing them for any age group nor presenting them at any time of the day or night since they believe that the corrupting means can have harmful influence on the persons of any age, not only on children.

Although people all over the land are divided into functional groups, the groups are in cooperation everywhere, and they present no unfriendly attitude towards each other. While the people who live in different areas keep the interesting differences of their cultures, in the way they prepare their food, the architecture of their buildings, and many of their customs related to daily activities, but they have no restrictive borders that would interfere with the ease of their traveling or visiting different parts of the land. Yet, there is no indiscriminate overpopulation of the favorite locations and cities because there are attractions and rules encouraging the people to spread out and live in the less crowded areas. The people of any location or group try very nicely to be rid of prejudice towards other decent groups and individuals, enjoying their friendship in spite of their cultural and other diversities.

The people of different religious practices do not insist on converting others to their own groups. Instead, they all try to be united together in being good to each other and doing what is right for the society in general. They take part in organized religious activities to encourage the whole society to follow the instructions given by God Almighty more appropriately while they insist on the fact that all of them believe in and worship The One And Only God, without accepting anybody or anything from this universe as partner to God, nor assigning to The Creator any human, animate, or inanimate face from our material world. They avoid insisting on the superlative importance of a selected prophet of theirs or emphasizing the favored status of their own people compared to all of the others. There the people of different religious practices discourage their preachers and religious teachers or leaders from dividing them, against the religious order, into groups with each group insisting on its own legitimacy and superiority.

As mentioned earlier, the degree of respect and support that the individuals receive in that land depends upon the adequacy of proper human qualities and not according to success in gaining control over a larger supply of the luxuries of this world or higher influence in worldly matters, nor by having exceptional physical qualities or some fascinating capabilities which are useless as a true measure of service to the society. Depending on the degree of their admirable and unselfish qualities, as well as their self-sacrifice in helping others, the people who live there gain positive points by way of being recognized or honored but get negative points for their selfish acts and their lack of concern for others. As a result, individuals are seriously discouraged from hoarding wealth for themselves since there is no honor but disrespect for mere wealth in that land. Still, as one can get positive recognition through helping the society, the wealthy individuals can get positive marks if they spend, as they can afford, from their wealth adequately to help the budget of the communities and those who may be in need. In this way they may be liked by the society for the greater volume of good deeds that they perform, rather than being a target of dislike and disrespect because of accumulating money for themselves. That society keeps from respecting or highly recognizing the persons who are in higher social positions or those who have more political power just because of their status, but again gives them respect depending on how good are their human qualities and how well they use their influence in serving the society.

The people of that land favor and support the workers who try to perform better, not those who only advertise effectively; the physicians who do what they feel is more appropriate for their patients and the communities, not the ones who take advantage of people's trust by doing what is not indicated and are better only in making money; the lawyers who are more honest in their service to the community, not the ones who make unfair settlements and cause punishment to the innocents; the politicians who try to do what is better for all, not those whose main intention is to secure their own positions at the expense of damage to the society; the speakers who say the truth, not those who only tell better jokes; and the persons who try to be truly productive, not those who waste the people's time with what is useless or at times even harmful, such as some unclean immoral entertainment which is detrimental to the society and its future.

Those people live not just for the moment but more for the future, and they do generally, not only what brings them temporary pleasure, but what gives them satisfaction for doing right. The young are pleased with their living wisely. They take advantage of what is correctly at their disposal of the pleasures for that age. They do not exhaust themselves by trying to get as much as possible of the temporary pleasures of right and wrong, as if this were the only period they would live in. In regard to romance, they control their desires with strength, keeping their commitments to those who will ethically and legally belong to them for that purpose at the right time.

The people of that land perform adequate physical work and take part in proper sport to improve the function of their minds and bodies. They have a greater tendency towards participating in sports rather than only being spectators. They enjoy healthy recreations and try courageously to avoid any harmful entertainment that can be a source of corruption to them or to others. They are considerate of the comfort in their communities. They do not attend activities that can disturb other people's peace of mind. They care about the tranquility of their surroundings and try to keep them as free as possible of noise pollution. They do not bother others with untimely blowing of the horn of their automobiles when some are resting in a residential area or letting the loud noise of their car radio or home stereo be a nuisance to other people. The doctors, nurses, and other employees and visitors in the medical facilities conscientiously keep the atmosphere quiet, which is needed for sensitive patients and their delicate feelings. The people are well in control of their emotions, and they refrain from making inappropriate loud noise even during their conversations. They try not to raise their voice to each other with rudeness, and they realize that, when one's voice is raised during the debates and discussions, or one uses bad language, or perhaps shows muscle or other means of physical power, one is presenting evidence of weakness of personality and lack of adequate strength of words.

In my dreamland there is minimal requirement for availability of officials engaged in law enforcement since people
generally follow the rules and laws of their locations conscientiously. In that land there is hardly any need for police, judges,
criminal lawyers, and jail personnel. Some volunteers among
the population of any locality, according to their knowledge,
career, education, and expertise, fulfill these services whenever
required. The whole society may be considered to be involved
in law enforcement. The professionals in these careers are often
busy with preventive measures, involved in giving lectures and
providing social service, or teaching children and the public
their community's rules and regulations for safer living. There
the people do not cause intentional damage to each other's
person or property, as individuals or as groups. Crimes and
criminals are almost nil. There are no fights and wars among
the people, as there exists no serious conflict of interests.
Everybody is generally concerned about the interests of the
others and the well-being of the whole society.

They consider **crime** intolerable and their society deserving
to be void of criminal acts. They deal harshly with criminals by
meting out severe physical punishment, evident to the public,
and without consideration of the criminal's wealth, social
status, or influence. Criminals are punished without undue
delay, perhaps within only a few days or weeks following the
presentation of adequate evidence and after a speedy trial.
Justice needs only reasonable certainty about the crime, and
time is not wasted in discussions over reasonable or unreasonable doubts. Of course, anybody who gives wrong witness
or has malice in accusing someone incorrectly is punished very
severely, too. They do not permit the argument that individuals
have inherent tendency towards serious wrongdoing, sexual
misconducts, criminal acts, or violent behavior because of their
genes or an acquired habit due to their past bitter experiences,
be a matter of consideration in their judgments. They show a
strong reaction to such faults such that anybody would be seriously discouraged from these involvements, no matter if that
person may or may not have some underlying obsessive com-
pulsive disorder forcing them towards these misbehaviors.

If an occasional crime takes place, the scene and the incident are not brought to the public's attention for entertainment, but left to responsible officials or authorities to deal with. On the other hand, severe swift punishment is brought to the society's notice. The punishment for wrongdoing and crime is much more severe in the case of those who take advantage of the confidence which is offered to them by the society because of their status. For example, if some physicians, some police officers, some politicians, some teachers, some judges, some lawyers, or some religious figures, having earned the trust of their communities, do wrong to the people purposely, they are punished more vigorously. In the case of criminal acts committed by young children or those severely affected by mental illness, who could not be considered totally responsible for their actions, they would adequately punish the parents or other responsible individuals as well. The people of that land believe this attitude towards crime and wrongdoing is a must if their society is to be protected from gradual deterioration and decay.

As needed, they have political system or systems in that land for proper management of the society's affairs. For those people it does not make a difference, no matter what kind of political regime is in force. The people and their government **trust each other and work together** sincerely towards improving the society's life. The people cooperate in each community and adequately follow the appropriate instructions of their proper officials and authorities. They obey the laws and help keep the governments functioning in an orderly manner without disregarding the rules or hurting the proper performance of their governments. People in authority, the elected and selected officials, and other individuals with political and financial clout use their privileges in the way of serving their communities and the society as a whole. They do not use their influence, as the case may be in parts of our present world, for satisfying their own interests against what is right for the people, nor do they oppress their people and the clients bitterly by show of force, at times, when they find the occasion for doing so while they are in a position of authority. They strive individually and in cooperation with each other to serve their communities and the whole society. They do not use their power for supporting one another for the purpose of reinforcing their authoritative bunch in confrontation with the innocent majority.

In that land those who have positions of influence behave as having the responsibility of serving the society, not as having the opportunity of abusing their privileges for dominating their communities unfairly and showing arrogance to the society. There the people do not give too much social privilege to those who have more authority for serving the society, so that they do not encourage others to try to gain access to those positions just for the luxury and privileges, instead of their honest will for service.

In that land individuals with whatever level of political power, members of the government, and any other officials with high influence, live like others in the open society and are **not separate from the people**, nor would they live with too much of luxury and extravagance. They trust their people because they are doing what is right for the society and are not involved in wrongdoing for which they would fear the people's disappointment. They also have very high confidence that their well-educated people are so nice and trustworthy that they would be safeguarding those people of authority, rather than being any threat to their security. Individuals who are responsible for setting the laws and the rules for the people perform with sincerity and honesty, doing what is to the society's advantage, not that they only consider what might benefit their favored groups, nor that they would be more concerned about their own future compared to what is right for all.

In that land the degree of individuals' success in advancing towards higher goals depends on their **honest performance** and not according to favors or the use of unofficial influence and inappropriate force of others in official dealings. Occasionally, persons who might favor the latter approach or behavior, which is wrong, would expect serious untoward consequences. There is no bribery nor any favoritism there.

The innocent people of that society are **equal in their rights**, no matter what social status they have, which family they belong to, or how much wealth they control. Each person feels embarrassed to make a recommendation to anyone else for doing some inappropriate favor with consideration of making an unfair exception or discrimination. In every aspect of their daily life and in dealing with other people and their business or profession and the products of their work, the great majority of people always keeps in consideration the **moral issues**, the ethical standards, and their family values. They regard these important points seriously when dealing with others. They reject the physician who has sexual misbehaviors, despite the skill and knowledge of the profession. They do not support the politician who is very efficient at work but has inappropriate addictions, nor the successful person of business and the champion in sports who have immoral behaviors. They boycott the publications which are full of inappropriate stories and writings or indecent pictures, and they do not watch or listen to the programs of the broadcasting services, the movies, and other presentations if they are not properly in harmony with decent social values. They do not buy the wrong products, even if there are some aspects of fun or pleasure attached to them.

In other words, the wonderful people of those communities, united together as the determined and powerfully effective members of the society, persist in fighting against evil and wicked individuals. They control their emotions in dealing with other people and the products of their work, rather than supporting them carelessly by having fun with what goes on while disregarding the advice of their conscience and moral values. In my dreamland no matter what system or systems of government might be in force, there exists a proper democracy for the people, but their freedom is guided in every aspect of the society's function by ethics and the moral or common religious values. They have majority rule generally in force, yet it does not mean that the people can decide about every simple or complicated issue. The majority selects or elects properly qualified individuals and groups or committees. Those experts and specialists, then with the use of their knowledge and expertise, make the required important decisions.

They support the better people and encourage them to do what is right, but they do not make a big issue of praising or admiring persons for their important achievements. Instead, they thank God Almighty, in appreciation of the occasions and opportunities, including the available human efforts and cooperations, that made those achievements possible. They do not build statues of or name streets, buildings, and locations after famous persons. The individuals of that land try to be good and do what is right for the society because they feel that is their duty, not that they try to show and exaggerate the importance of what they have done in expectation of receiving more admiration and higher recognition.

Their laws protect the **freedom of speech for expression of opinions** and ideas, but not with application of rude words and unclean discussions or with inappropriate body or gesture presentations that would be against decent human values. It is forbidden there to present to the public what can damage the society's lifestyle, virtues, and safety, for example through promotion by the publishing and broadcasting industries of sexual misconduct, crime, violence, or other misbehaviors.

The people are generally content with their life. There is no serious depression affecting anybody's mind, and there is no suicide in that land. Individuals are so concerned about the society that they are happier when they feel they are needed by others and they can help them. Their **joy** is not derived from their ability to find clever ways of abusing the opportunities to receive greater privileges from others while, without having proper excuse or disability, doing less and less true service to the society. The people are generally **pleasant** in their dealings with others in the society, particularly offering their support to the better individuals. They do not have the habit that each person demonstrates kindness when needing other people's favors but stops being nice to them when there is the feeling of not needing them any more.

The news media and other means of public information in that land do not encourage their communities to have **any kind of group prejudice**, nor do they stimulate hate and dislike among the groups.

In my dreamland the calculation and collection of **income tax** are according to how the money has been earned, expecting low payment from the money earned through decent, productive businesses or professions and very high taxation on the income which is from parasitic and useless performances.

The people of that land are nice to **animals**, and in keeping pets they do not cause an animal to suffer for their own pleasure. They keep the pets only to the extent of their capability to look after them humanely and they encourage the children and grown-ups always to remember that pets are animals and that we should avoid having such intimacy between them and our living conditions that we lose our own proper human cleanliness. They do hunting and fishing for the purpose of proper use of the animals such as eating them or for scientific work and research, but they do not hurt, injure, or kill the animals just for having fun or for making use of their parts as decorations or as unnecessary decorative clothing and other objects.

They do not have improper **discrimination** in that land when offering positions and opportunities to individuals. When people are asked questions about their particulars at the time of completing a registration or filing of an application, they may be asked about their qualifications, the languages they speak, and their date of birth, but unless it is necessary for a specific reason, they are not questioned about their race or nationality since all are residents of this planet and belong to the human race.

Individuals who live in that land are generally looking forward to their own **old age** with excitement and optimism. They expect it to be a period of their life when they are possibly able to spend their time more easily on what they prefer to do, with fewer scheduled responsibilities but more free time to do as they please while receiving proper attention from the society and having more securities and privileges available to them, depending on how well their younger years have been spent in properly serving the society. They realize that at old age the simple pleasures of life can be many times more enjoyable for us when we know that some young ones who are very dear to us have those pleasures available to them, even if many of those we cannot engage in personally. The disabilities or difficulties related to old age are tolerated by these people; they accept them with grace as part of what they cope with, in their joy for having had the occasion of reaching that special period of life. Since older people in that land generally have the tendency of showing contentment and securities of that age, their young ones also expect that period of life happily and with confidence.

In my dreamland the **practice of medicine** has been simplified, at the same time that it is offered at the best level of quality. There the patients generally receive first class medical care from physicians, nurses, and other medical personnel, who try to deliver the care that they would expect to receive themselves if they were the patients. Among the nurses, those who waste time in nonprofessional personal engagements at work, when they are supposed to help their patients, are few. Nurses generally enjoy the time that they spend in caring for the ones who need their expertise.

The physicians' main concern in the delivery of medical service is to offer the best quality of care to the patients and their communities, not only the volume of work they get to do and the amount of money collected and piled up as a result. They have time to listen to their patients and time to answer the questions of the right number of patients they may be able to help properly. The physicians are generally so conscientious that patients trust them wholeheartedly, and the team consisting of the concerned medical personnel, the cooperative patient, and the patient's close and affectionate relatives, works together and helps each other in the struggle to obtain the best result from treatments. They try to solve medical and related problems as well as possible with their mutual concern and cooperation without blaming one another inappropriately at the times they are disappointed with the outcomes.

The cost of the health care is provided by the budget assigned for this purpose while well-affording communities can spend easily and the people support that budget comfortably, according to their individual incomes. Each person's medical and related expenses are covered adequately for the best available care unless for the problems resulted from that individual's wrongdoing, such as sexual misbehaviors, substance abuse, or guilty involvement in criminal acts. They do not waste the society's resources in providing extra expense for unnecessary administrative services above the very basic amount that is needed. They prioritize medical expenses of that society accurately, spending the right amount in the proper place, emphasizing disease prevention and improvement of hygiene and lifestyle of their individuals and the communities.

They do not waste much of their time and resources in the struggle to extend the misery of the terminally ill and the last days of the ones who are suffering at old age from a difficult state of suspension between their ailments and the treatments while they are ready to have that last uncomfortable waiting over so that they can finish the closing part of this temporary period of their existence with dignity. They realize that for conservation and continuation of proper life for the human generations on earth, their communities ought to observe some sensible rules regarding their lifestyle, health care, and **population control.**

They know that if their society did not observe family planning for keeping the population at optimum on earth, the population explosion of the human species would cause grave imbalance of life on the planet with extinction of the majority of the other species on one hand, and propagation of the diseases related to overcrowding, starvation, pollutions, and as a result, a variety of the complications threatening the survival of our generations on the other hand.

The people of that land do not insist on treating every sickness. They know they are not to disturb aggressively the **balance of life** that exists on earth even though our sentiments may not appreciate some of the factors that control this delicate balance. We can observe in the world of animals, that for having a more sustainable life to continue on the surface of this planet, there is generally more tendency for the feeble and incapable to fall behind and become prey of other animals or succumb to sickness and death. There is also a general balance that is kept between the different sections of life, for example between animals and plants, through their availability and need, their survival being interdependent.

The people of my dreamland try to offer means of comfort and relief from suffering to the sick, but they keep from wasting the society's resources in treating some of the diseases which are effectively cleansing the society from those who are expected to continue in a poor health and difficult state of life. They pay attention to the fact that if they proceed to influence the life of human species in a way that is against the harmony which has been provided in nature, they can cause disaster for mankind and other life on this planet:

- if they search for better treatments and ways of extending the life of every individual who even has poor quality of life and grave outlook for self and the society;
- if they are successful in finding ways of elongating the average life span of people, with gradual increase of the proportion of the old and feeble individuals with poor quality of life who are of no positive effect for others compared to the ones who constitute the productive sector of the society;
- if they keep treating every disease with a variety of natural and synthetic remedies and they generate with an escalating speed new and more aggressive types of microorganisms and diseases which are more resistant to the available treatments;
- if they cause to increase the population of the world, gradual multiplying of overcrowded cities and locations; and
- if, as a result, they continue to cause a variety of pollutions, making life intolerable for our own species and impossible for many other plants and animals that become extinct due to our population explosion.

Then our human race will be faced with more and more disasters, affecting very large masses of people, such as the epidemic diseases with exceedingly virulent and resistant microorganisms, famine, rebellions, wars, and a variety of sufferings that we may not even be able to anticipate nor have any way of preventing, once the miserable and unbearable condition of life on earth becomes irreversible.

The people of my dreamland consider **family as the cell or unit of life** for the whole society. They realize that for having a healthy society the individual cells need to be in good condition, as the life of the society starts from within the families. In that society two persons of opposite gender make marriage vows to become committed to one another for as long as the two of them live. This is done usually at an early age, if needed with the financial and other supports by their parents and the concerned communities, with the intention of forming a family unit and raising very good children. Then, as time goes on, their attachment together and their need for each other can become deeper, their association sweeter, and the family unit stronger.

There is no promiscuity in that land, and **romance** exists only between those who have committed themselves to each other. If occasionally some individuals have romantic involvement prior to the time that they are ready for their permanent commitment, this would be between the young person and preferably a barren old one, so that their commitment can be easily terminated without serious emotional attachment. In this way there would be less possibility of complications, such as communicable diseases or unwanted pregnancies, and also far less detrimental influence on later permanent married life.

People there accept the fact that for a healthy society to function and progress correctly there should exist a proper and durable attachment, contractual, familial, emotional, and spiritual, between the two persons of the opposite gender, who live together with a continuously reinforced attraction that keeps the family unit in good form. With that comes the possibility of having the children who are raised and educated while in touch with the loving and caring attendance of the two parents, towards forming the future generation with continuation of a healthy progress for the society. They realize that for this goal to be reached, the cooperation of the whole society is needed.

They follow many delicate and at times difficult rules to make this pleasantly clean way of life a practical trend for their individuals. They do not mix together the people of the opposite gender who are not close relatives, whether young or old, in conditions and circumstances that can promote lustful temptations and unethical romance. This is true at their schools and other centers for education, where they are serious and academically oriented rather than wasting time in romantic involvements; at places of work, where they concentrate on achieving better productivity; and while in their other activities and social gatherings, though they enjoy very well what they do under the umbrella of faith, ethics, and morality, yet keeping safe from the vicious rays of evil temptations that can give them temporary and false happiness and ruin their future with a variety of complications.

They know that it is not proper to mix the youngsters of the opposite gender freely together, dressed inappropriately and without adequate adult supervision, then to ask them not to have courtship; nor to let them have close friendship, ignoring religious instructions and moral family values, but ask them to avoid a sexual relationship; nor to let them get involved in un-ethical romance and ask them to desist from pregnancies or avoid getting affected by diseases and other related defaults and complications; nor should we let them have a filthy promiscuous life but expect them to get married later with a permanent covenant void of unfaithfulness or divorce.

Those people make their adolescents comprehend the fact that as far as sexual pleasures are concerned, it should be noted that when people respect and practice proper religious and ethical restrictions which are placed upon their sight, their words, their attire and their behavior in the society, they may continue to enjoy more fully their own lawful spouse and go on having future pleasures. However, those who do things without observing the proper boundaries will be ensnared in more un-ethical acts in order to be pleased and will possibly get into more and more unlawful and improper involvements with less and less enjoyment.

They understand that if they expose their bodies indecently to be more attractive in the society, and if they inappropriately touch, kiss, hug, and flirt, then they are going to have more of the wrong relationships, and they will need more of that to give them any satisfaction, resulting in more serious problems in the society in relation to people's sexuality, family problems and stress, or other emotional complications. In that land women, young or old, cover their beauty in public decently, and men avoid showing any part of their body indecently, both genders trying more and more to be decent in the way they talk, dress, and behave, rather than having a tendency towards showing more of their skin and attracting and charming others in public.

Their broadcasting and publishing or other related in-dustries follow the same rule, so that they do not present or print indecent words or scenes and pictures for their communities. Instead, they encourage the individuals to avoid exposing parts of their body in public or expressing verbal or physical gestures that stimulate lustful temptations. Each person lowers the gaze and tries not to look at or touch, with lustful intent, other than the person one is allowed to for that purpose with appropriate covenant and commitments.

In this way, when people get married, the two spouses are so attached to one another and to their mutual family unit that each of them can trust the other one wholeheartedly since neither one of them would become attracted to anybody else for romance, regardless of whatever physical or other characteristics, and each of the two will have confidence that the other party evinces the same strong marital bond.

In that society the bond of marriage is not only being supported by the two persons who are joined to each other through it, but that bridge of connection involves the families and communities, who effectively reinforce it through their concern, and it is strengthened with the whole society's expectations and the efforts which are in the right direction, so that it is not like a flimsy and temporary passageway made over a ditch to connect a few houses together, but like a sturdy and long-lasting bridge built, reinforced, and continuously maintained through the concern and interests of the populations of the large cities located on the two sides of the river. With such a strong marital attachment, any two spouses in that land trust one another and the society. They respect the faith and faithfulness, enjoying their clean relationship, with long-lasting pleasures, in a well-organized family unit, looking forward with optimism to a bright future, rather than taking advantage of a transient romance with deep feeling of sadness and sorrow that as their life and age would advance, they are not going to be able to continue having that temporary superficial luxury but instead to expect serious complications in their future.

Since most of the individuals of my dreamland avoid having any romantic involvement prior to their marriage, the spouses try very hard and happily to solve any marital problems and make willingly the needed compromises so that the marriage works, as they believe that the one family unit they have is the best possible one that they could ever have in their lifetime. The parents and other responsible elders teach the children of both genders from very early age the modesty and the rules of affinity for being noble and chaste. They help them get married early in life, before having a chance of becoming corrupted with promiscuity. Since most of those people have their romance with only one spouse, their bond of affection, when married, becomes strong very fast as they adapt to each other quickly, even if the process of selection has been greatly influenced by the advice from their concerned elders.

The young do not use the excuse of looking for a suitable match while indulging in promiscuity, since they wisely understand that the more variety they taste in romance, the greater the possibility for their displeasure with their marriage, with a higher probability of looking for excuses or reasons to break it up. They agree that the strength of their attachment to one another after marriage is much less related to their preexisting conditions and qualities than to their sincere willingness and desire to follow and adapt to each other's needs and wishes.

In the families of that land usually one spouse is the head of the household, with more responsibilities for providing the means of sustenance for the unit and more authority in making difficult decisions. The other one mainly takes care of the home environment, especially spending time with any young child at home. The parents support their children willingly and with pleasure. In turn, the children, when grown up, care for the elders with concern and dignity. The parents in that land have adequate authority over their children and help them learn to follow proper discipline while maturing in life. At the same time, they offer plenty of affection and emotional attachment to the children.

In my dreamland the **members of the family unit** all feel the need for mutual association for having a pleasant success in their performance while being emotionally attached together with such a strong affection that each of them senses the confidence in belonging to that family unit, regardless of any distracting temptations or even in the face of interferences by others in the society. The two spouses accept their differences from each other and the fact that their responsibilities in the family are not all alike. In this way they feel more in need of each other, without comparing the importance or the value of their functions. They agree that, for example, the strong attitude of one and the delicate and gentle touch of the other one are both needed in conjunction for their joint venture and mutual success in dealing with problems. Many a time the gentle approach can nicely solve some difficult problems.

This can be compared to what goes on in our mouth, where cooperation and harmony are needed between the different parts and functions during mastication of food. Some brittle food particles, which could otherwise injure tongue and throat with sharp edges, are broken to pieces by our teeth, with the indispensable help and manipulations offered by the tongue; on the other hand, a piece of hard candy that can break the tooth, may with patience and the gentle action of saliva be dissolved completely and swallowed with ease.

The people of my dreamland consider the **education of children** as a most valuable investment towards securing the future happiness and well-being of their society. Having proper education and the best quality of educators available for all of the children and other willing individuals who are in need of learning receives the highest of priorities in that land. They help their children acquire the love of learning. With the dedication of the parents and the school faculties and with their mutual cooperative work, such a pleasantly efficient atmosphere of education is prepared that school attendance and studying are fun for those youngsters, in a proper academic way, without offering too many sports or other activities as entertainment that can distract their attention from studies and waste their valuable time.

The people of that land are so beautifully nurtured with different aspects of education during their growing years that they have in them a strong attachment to a variety of essential human qualities which are needed for their society's excellent functioning and have satisfied, according to their individual talents, their learning capabilities so that they would be rightly productive for their communities. From the time of early youth, they have accepted the fact that the best way to quit the abuse of any of the addictives, such as smoking, alcoholic beverages, and drugs other than for medical use, is not ever to have the very first experience of using them. They take part in an adequate amount of healthy physical exercises or sports and participate in proper competitions, yet at the conclusion of each competition they do not make a big issue of the result, but rather of the efforts having been spent to do it right. Neither do the winners show off with a big celebration nor do the losers display grimace and sorrow. People do not submit to wrongful acts and excesses with the excuse of celebrating an occasion. They have learned how to control their emotions adequately in happiness and sorrow.

They present in their lifestyle and they support with their daily activities the better human qualities and social values such as: honesty with fairness, humility with kindness, faith with righteousness, trust with truthfulness, hygiene with cleanliness, courage with bravery, care with politeness, and the other characteristics of people of class and quality. They have become so attentive and understanding, through proper education, that they are not easily fooled into believing in what is false or manipulated to do what is wrong. They generally recognize what the truth is and are determined to do right. They are not oppressed by the arrogant, and they do not support the wrongdoers, no matter what social status they have; nor are they impressed by mere wealth, worldly fame, authority, or material luxuries and extravagance, but they respect the better human qualities and promote goodwill and what can be considered true service to the society.

Those well-educated people are united together in cooperation for the propagation of good and their constant fight against evil. During the early years of life they have received much affection from their attentive elders, hence as adults they are well-balanced individuals emotionally. They have been taught how they can happily control their desires in the way of doing what is right and how to be pleased after suppressing their emotions, when needed to do so, in favor of timely application of their wisdom and logic. Therefore, the youth in that land advance through their adolescence with a sense of security and optimism together with strong responsibility towards their society and its future, getting ready to apply their well-prepared capabilities by way of serving the society and hopefully improving the living conditions of their fellow human beings.

55

The Example of a Tree

In the beginning of the book I made a comparison of the content of this book, including the variety of the subjects or discussions, to the branches of a tree. By the time you have reached this latter part of the book, I hope you can put these branches together in a more organized fashion in your thoughts, forming a useful tree with strong roots, sturdy trunk and beautifully arranged branches. The root is our firm faith in God Almighty, with total commitment to follow the orders given by God. Through our belief in The One Supreme Authority, without accepting any other association or partnership, or making human or material idols for each of our groups, we can promote more unity among the residents of this planet, rather than create disparity. The trunk of the tree represents our strong dedication to serve the society as a whole. While performing our responsibilities, through this dedication we may practically show how one can gain pleasure from sacrificing some comfort of self for the sake of providing privileges to others. A tree formed in this way can hopefully produce delicious and nourishing fruits. The fruits, which are the contents of these pages, may be considered delicious if you find them suitable to the taste of your mind, and nourishing when used in serving our society and in improving its future.

One of the most important tasks of this writing is to unite together the better people of our society all over the world. Each reader of the book will probably disagree with some parts of the writing at first glance. The better people of our world are not all united together in one group, but they are separated in different religious and other groups. This book is intended to be for all of them and is not to please one group of people and meet their viewpoints only. It is needed for all to keep their emotions controlled and seek some logical compromises in order to make it possible to find a decent common ground for all to be united there. Otherwise, if the groups keep insisting on differentiating their beliefs and ideas, while empowering these with emotions and prejudice, the better people of our world are going to continue hurting each other as groups, under the influence of ignorant people who keep them separate with conflict of worldly interests and persistent unfriendliness.

56

Closing Comments

In this book my simple understanding of some important matters related to the life of our society has been presented to the readers. In this presentation, I have tried to be frank, mentioning sincerely what my personal beliefs are.

I may have made many mistakes in the writing of the text or may have been wrong in some of the suggestions. It is not a holy book, nor claimed to be perfect.

I do not claim any power of prophecy or possession of some exceptional qualification. I have done good and bad or right and wrong, as others may have. I am not trying to establish a new way of life, nor form a gang or a cult. I am simply trying to explain how important it is that we encourage all members of our society to be more and more considerate of the future of the life of mankind on this planet; to be concerned about the well-being of our society collectively, not only a group or some groups thereof; to adhere to some logical principles and pay attention to what is right for long-lasting future satisfactions, rather than the temporary pleasures of the moment with consequentially detrimental effects; to be pleased with what gives comfort to others, rather than having interest in personal benefit at the expense of their discomfort; to search for and join in friendship, the others who feel the same way as they try to perform their proper share of service to our society all over the world, ignoring the unimportant differences that may exist among us.

When enough people of different nations with the aforementioned unselfish intentions cooperate to serve the society, as they would qualitatively and quantitatively constitute the dominant human and humane guiding force, they may very well succeed in achieving their goals, regardless of what lands they live in, what systems of government are ruling in their areas, or what apparent groups they may belong to.

Let us hope there may come a day when most of the people who live on this planet help one another, everyone doing more good for the society than for self. They would cooperate in conserving this planet's health, with the integrity of life on its surface, using deliberate effort to improve it. They would be law-abiding people, following the rules of the land they live in and the instructions given by the proper responsible authorities, yet, when needed, they would succeed in changing or improving the laws of the nations for the betterment of the future of the society as a whole until all groups of mankind on earth can live together in peace, friendship, trust, cooperation, and confidence. Then shall they truly feel united as one common race, all being human; living in one common country, all inhabitants of the planet earth; and having one common religion, all worshipping, believing in, and praying to The One And Only God.

Index